Cover Photos:

Top: The boxcar from 1899 near Georgenthal, State of Thuringia Germany.

Bottom: The *Fagen Fighters WWII Museum* in Granite Falls, MN, proudly displays the restored Holocaust boxcar. A large educational exhbit is a major component of this world-class museum.

For Christine and Gitta

The Holocaust Boxcar

A Powerful Admonition Against Anti-Semitism

Friedhelm Caspari and Joachim Reppmann

ISBN 978-0-9912758-2-3

2. Edition May 2017

© Copyright 2016 by Stoltenberg Institute for German-American Forty-Eighter Studies
103 N. Orchard St.; Northfield, MN; 55057; USA

yogireppmann@gmail.com — www.Moin-Moin.us

Benjamin Parsell, Minnesota, Webmaster, bsparsell@gmail.com

Dietrich Eicke, Bad Oldesloe, www.eickeweb.de, designed *moin* Logo.

Georg Wawerla, Kiel, www.studio38-kiel.de, designed 1848er Logo.

Table of Contents

Preface	9
Introduction	11
1840 – A Driving Force for Growth in Germany: The Railroad	15
19th Century – Biedermeier and Fomanticism	15
1813/1848 – The German National Flag: Black-Red-Gold	18
1848-1857 – Waves of Emigrants to North America	19
1840 – Anti-Semitism in the 19th Century	21
1871 – The Founding of the German Empire	21
1871 to 1914 - The Citizen as "Underling"	23
1879 – Anti-Semitism Becomes "Socially Acceptable"	24
1914 to 1918 – The First World War	25
1919 to 1933 – The Weimar Republic	30
1933 to 1945 - The Nazi Dictatorship of the Third Reich	31
1933 – With the Blessing of the Churches	33
1933 – Books Burn in German Cities *(Flensburg, p.35)*	34
1938 – The Night of the Pogroms, November 9	37
1941 to 1945 – The Holocaust / Shoah	39
1939 – The Railroad as Death Transport	40
1942 – The Final Decision to Murder all Jews	42
1933 to 1945 – The Horror of the Concentration Camps	44
1933 to 1945 – Resistance and the Rescue of Jews	46
1936 to 1939 – The Bombing War begins in Spain	53
1939 to 1945 – Expansion of the Bombing War	53
1944 – D-Day, the Beginning of the End of the War	57
May 1945 – The End of the War: Surrender and Liberation	57
1933 to 1946 – Emigration, Exile, Flight, and Expulsion	58
Flensburg: The Last Stop of Nazi-Deutschland	59
1945 and 1946 – Further Consequences in the German-Danish Region	66
2015 – A Wave of Refugees Surprises Germany	67
Appendices	71
Contributors and *Danke*	96

Preface

*"Whoever refuses to remember the inhumanity
is prone to new risks of infection."*

"You must know everything that happened then, and why it happened." This is the appeal made by Auschwitz survivor Esther Bejarano to present and future generations. In doing so, she issues an injunction not only to Germans but to all people: to go beyond remembering and memorializing the millions of victims of National Socialist tyranny by understanding its historical context.

On May 8, 1985, the 40th anniversary of German's unconditional surrender to Allied forces which ended World War II in Europe, Richard von Weizsäcker, then President of the Federal Republic of Germany, spoke out against forgetting:

"It is not a case of coming to terms with the past. That simply cannot be done. It is not possible to make it 'undone'. However, anyone who closes his eyes to the past is blind to the present. Whoever refuses to remember the inhumanity is prone to new risks of infection."

For the Germany of the 19th and 20th centuries, one stone of prejudice was built on top of another. The resulting accumulation of hatred, intolerance, aggression, exclusionary political decisions, and merciless militarism rose to a peak, then unparalleled in human history. This fateful combination ultimately led to nationally sanctioned mass murder.

In a manner akin to time-lapse photography, this publication attempts to make clear how the World Wars of the 20th century and the deadly machinery of the Hitler regime arose and developed. The Nazis' system of violence, with its horribly dedicated apparatus for the focus annihilation of the Jewish people, members of opposition parties, and minorities, "lives not worth living", was not an accident of history but the insistent consequence of political and societal forces. The Holocaust boxcar discussed in this book, one of the many different kinds of rail-cars used to deliver more than 4,000,000 Jews to their death.

Let us quote Richard von Weizsäcker once again, from a speech heard then around the world: "The Jewish nation remembers and will always remember. We seek reconciliation as human beings. Precisely for this reason we must understand that there can be no reconciliation without remembrance. The experience of millions of deaths is part of the very being of every Jew in the world, not only because people cannot forget such atrocities, but also because remembrance is part of the Jewish faith." Quoting the ancient Jewish sages, von Weizsäcker added: "Seeking to forget makes exile all the longer; the secret of redemption lies in remembrance."
(For the complete speech, see Appendix 1, p. 71.)

Georgenthal, State of Thuringia, from left to right: Ron and Diane Fagen, Minister President Christine Lieberknecht, and Yogi Reppmann, September 24, 2015.

Introduction

The period of National Socialism in Germany and the horrors of the Hitler regime cannot be understood apart from the political and societal developments that preceded them. The events that took place between the wars and during the Nazi dictatorship have been analyzed, illuminated, and described many times. Literature on the structure of the Nazi system and its leading figure, the "populist" Adolf Hitler, has been published extensively and in many languages. For the first time, however, we are offering for American and German readers a fact book, "The Holocaust Boxcar—A Powerful Admonition Against Anti-Semitism" that briefly explains the most important developments in Germany during the nineteenth and twentieth centuries.

In the fall of 2015, an abandoned German boxcar dating from the year 1899 began its long journey halfway around the world from the Thuringian Forest to the *Fagen Fighters World War II Museum* in Granite Falls, Minnesota. Joachim "Yogi" Reppmann learned of the boxcar from his uncle Peter Prass from Gera, who had spent thirty-four years working on the railroad behind the Iron Curtain in East Germany.

Having teamed with Diane Fagen, president of the museum, Yogi arranged to have this horrific reminder of the Holocaust transported to the museum in Granite Falls. The boxcar had originally been used as a normal rail vehicle for merchandise, but eventually carried victims identified for elimination by the Nazis to the concentration camp at Auschwitz. On May 21, 2016, the Fagen Fighters Museum opened its Holocaust Boxcar and POW exhibit, the most recent addition to its historical aviation displays. In its present location, the boxcar serves as a "lesson in history" and should be understood by the public as such. In the context of the Fagen Fighters exhibition, the present compendium would be highly appropriate as reading material in American and German high school and college programs, where it would offer an instructive commentary on some of the most cataclysmic events in German history. Today this topic is more relevant than ever, considering the lack of understanding, the hatred and intolerance among populist movements and agitators that has developed in connection with the recent waves of refugees worldwide.

As the war ended, Berlin lay in ruins and Hitler had committed suicide. In the first days of May 1945, the north German city of Flensburg wrote a chapter of its own history. This city on the border with Denmark received thousands of German refugees from the eastern territories and people who had been freed from concentration camps. At the same time, however, hundreds of top-brass Nazis went into hiding in the city, which became the new "capital of the Reich" for a few days. A television documentation of this unusual complex of events in Flensburg during the final days of the war, was produced in March 2017 by Stephan Witthöft, Erfurt, SALVE MEDIA; *A Flensburg Perspective: Erna de Vries and the Holocaust Boxcar.*
(www.Moin-Moin.us 'Videos')

Grand Opening of the Holocaust and POW Boxcar Exhibit, on May 21st, 2016, Granite Falls, MN; note the embroidered map of Schleswig-Holstein from 1944 at the lower left.

May 21st, 2016, Grand Opening in western Minnesota, Aaron and Traci Fagen with Yogi Reppmann.

Charles Fodor, a Hungarian Holocaust survivor, and Steve Hunegs, the executive director of the Jewish Community Relations Council; Granite Falls, MN, on May 21st, 2016.

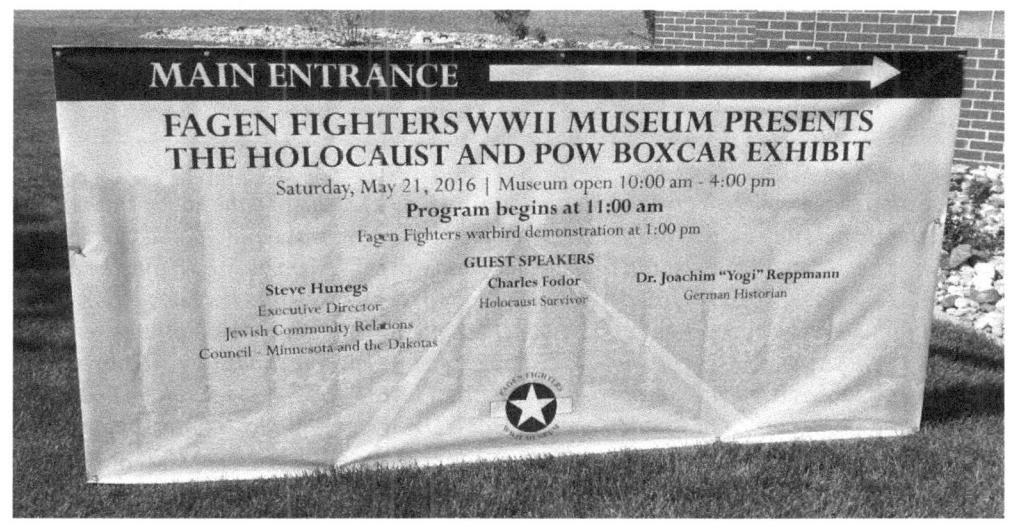

Approximately one thousand interested Americans attended the moving and educational mega-event.

www.fagenfightersWWIImuseum.org

The above map is a gift of Gitta and Yogi Reppmann's of May 21st, 2016 to the Fagen Fighters WWII Museum: Here is the story behind the gift. The map pictured above was embroidered by Käthe Benkwitz, who had been a head nurse south of Flensburg, and was passed on to us by a friend. Käthe died at the age of 92, having been married for only ONE day in her life; she and her husband had been married during WWII over the phone, and he was subsequently killed in action. Käthe never married again. In 1944 Käthe served as a nurse in France and cared for Field Marshall Erwin Rommel who was in a military hospital as a result of severe head injuries. On July 17th, 1944, weeks after D-Day, he had been traveling from the SS tank headquarters in France, when his driver lost control of the car and crashed into a tree following an attack by a Spitfire. As head nurse, Käthe was in charge of sitting at Rommel's bedside during the night. It was then that she embroidered the map of Schleswig-Holstein, her home state and ours. Because of Rommel's involvement in an attempt to assassinate Hitler, he was given the choice by Hitler of committing suicide and receiving a State Funeral, or of being executed. His only son, Manfred, fifteen years old at the time, learned of this choice minutes before his father's suicide.

1840 – A Driving Force for Growth in Germany: The Railroad

The industrial revolution in Germany: The period of time from 1830 to 1873 is considered the phase of pre- and early industrialization, the industrial "take off" in Germany. This is followed by more intensive industrialization during the German Empire, with emphasis on the coal and steel industry and the construction of railroads. This is in contrast to the greater importance of the textile industry in Great Britain, the country where industrialization was pioneered.

The railroad is the most powerful agent of growth in Germany: between 1850 and 1890 approximately 25% of all investments flow into this sector, more than those for trade or industry. In 1840 the railroad network is already approximately 580 kilometers long.

Only five years earlier, on December 7, 1835, railroad operation began with a short run from Nuremberg to Fürth. The Englishman William Wilson, the first locomotive engineer in Germany, completed the maiden voyage in the legendary locomotive "Adler" ("Eagle"). The Ludwigs Railroad Company, the operator of the first German rail line, adopted the English system. The first economically significant line, a 71 mile (115 kilometer) stretch between Leipzig and Dresden, was opened in 1837.

19th Century – Biedermeier and Romanticism

Society and culture in the German lands of the 19th century are characterized by sentiments in opposition to the revolutionary movement of that period. This is the time of Biedermeier and Romanticism. The name "Biedermeier" refers to art and culture in middle-class society between 1815 and 1848, including music performed at home, interior design, and fashion in clothing; the literature of this period is often described as "unadventurous" or "conservative."

The cultural epoch of Romanticism, from the end of the 18th century until well into the 19th, incorporates art, literature, and music. In painting, Late Romanticism lasts until the end of the 19th century; in music, until the beginning of the 20th century (Gustav Mahler, Richard Strauss).

At the societal level, flights into the idyllic and the private sphere are typical. In contrast, the political realm is dominated by the principle of restoration, resulting from the end of the Napoleonic period and the Congress of Vienna. Well-known literary figures of this politically reactionary and culturally Romantic period are Georg Büchner and Heinrich Heine[1].

While the middle class withdraws into the idyllic, radical changes are taking place in Germany. The year 1848 brings with it the "March Revolution," an open rebellion against the dictatorship of the monarchies and the aristocratic ruling class, following the example of the revolutionary developments in France and other European countries. As early as 1817, at the Wartburgfest

---

1. Heinrich Heine was born into a Jewish family and converted to Protestantism in 1825; a quotation from his tragedy "Almansor" (1821) prefigures the proscriptions of art and literature as well as the murder of Jews in the Nazi period: "... where they burn books, they will finally burn human beings as well." In May of 1933, the burning of literary works by writers banned by the Nazis took place, and ten years later Nazi criminals gassed and incinerated millions of people (cf. the following chapters).

near Eisenach, students from 36 individual German states demand freedom and unity. Later on, as a result of the "Carlsbad Decrees,"[2] they end up in prison in great numbers. Three decades later, many of these former Wartburgfest participants become the first and leading representatives in the Paulskirche Parliament.

The Hambacher Fest

The Hambacher Fest of 1832, at Hambach Castle as well as in Neustadt an der Haardt, is also considered one of the culminating points of middle-class opposition during the period of the Restoration. The participants' demands for national unity, freedom, and sovereignty of the people had their roots in the resistance to the reactionary endeavors of the German Federation (established in 1815).

The actual revolution in the German principalities and duchies begins in the Grand Duchy of Baden and spreads to the other states of the German Federation. From Berlin to Vienna, the revolutionaries force the establishment of liberal governments. The monarchs of the individual states agree to such political freedoms only because they are afraid of a reign of terror such as happened in France, but none of these aristocrats is whole-heartedly in favor of them.

The goal of the democratic movement is a nation with a parliamentary constitution that encompasses all the German-speaking lands. In order to prepare for this, liberal and democratic politicians from the smaller states gather at a "pre-parliament" in Heidelberg on March 5, 1848. As before, the liberals are in favor of the monarchy, but a monarchy supplemented by an elected parliament; the democrats, however, argue for a republic without a monarchy. A planned national assembly is to resolve this basic question and establish a constitution. The elections for this national assembly take different forms in the individual states, but everywhere only adult males have the right to vote. The final result is the first German parliament, with approximately 400 representatives who meet in the Paulskirche in the free city of Frankfurt am Main.

Rescinding the Reforms

At the same time, in late summer of 1848, state resistance is already beginning. The major powers, Prussia and Austria, proceed with violence against the democratic revolutionary movement. As a symbol of the monarchists' opposition, the Prussian king Friedrich Wilhelm IV refuses to accept the mandate of the national assembly. Previous to this, on March 28, 1849, he had been elected Emperor of the Germans. The constitution, ratified as the basis of a unified national state, is also rejected by the monarchies. In this constitution, freedom of the press and freedom to emigrate are included as basic rights.

---

2. The conferences of ministers in Carlsbad from August 6 to 31, 1819, in which the most influential states of the German Federation took part, deliberated and decided on measures concerning the surveillance of and opposition to liberal and national tendencies in post-Napoleonic Germany. Carlsbad (Czech: Karlovy Vary) belonged to the Habsburg Empire and as a spa was well-suited for portraying these secret meetings simply as private gatherings of diplomats and ministers, thereby concealing them from the public eye. The decrees came into being under the aegis of the legendary Austrian Foreign Minister and later state chancellor Metternich. The trigger was the fear of revolution that prevailed at the German courts. The justification for the Carlsbad Decrees was the murder on March 23, 1819 of the writer and Russian General Consul August von Kotzebue by Karl Ludwig Sand, a theology student and university fraternity member. The immediate cause of the decrees, however, were the riots at the beginning of August 1819, at which, for the first time since the Middle Ages, anti-Semitic outbreaks of violence had taken place in major German cities and had extended as far as Copenhagen and Amsterdam.

Soon the royal and princely houses retract the reforms they had promised and dissolve the parliaments in the individual states. In the process, the 23-year-old Viennese "waltz king" Johann Strauss Junior falls out of favor with the Austrian emperor Franz Joseph I because of certain pieces, such as the "Freedom Songs Waltz" and the "Revolution March," that he had composed for the revolutionaries.

From the fall of 1848 there are renewed revolutionary flare-ups, as the freedom fighters in Baden, Saxony, and the Bavarian Palatinate rebel. The situation is now similar to a civil war; Prussian and Austrian troops put down the uprisings with force, spelling the end of the revolutionary and democratic movement. The decade following the failed March revolution is known as the period of reaction. All parties and political organizations are now banned.

In the Duchy of Schleswig, which is part of the Danish royal house, particular events have been taking place. As early as 1840, German as well as Danish liberal nationalists intensify their efforts to gain political influence. The conflict breaks out into the open in the March revolution of 1848. A provisional government is declared in Kiel, demanding the acceptance of a unified Schleswig-Holstein into the German Federation. At the same time a liberal nationalist government is appointed in Copenhagen, with the intention of incorporating the Duchy of Schleswig constitutionally into the Kingdom of Denmark, thus separating the area from German Holstein. The irreconcilability of the opposing German and Danish positions leads to the Schleswig-Holstein uprising, in which the German side attempts in vain to end Danish sovereignty.

The societies of Prussia, Austria, and the other smaller German-language states withdraw more and more into middle-class life. This is essentially their passive response to the failed democratic movement. Still, the authorities and military powers of the German Federation continue with their saber rattling; after the collapse of the rebels come the German-Danish War (1864), the German-Austrian War (1866; also known as the German War), and the German-French War (1870-71).

1813/1848 – The German National Flag: Black-Red-Gold

Germany's flag has no official name, but is simply referred to as "Black-Red-Gold." Also in use is the synonym "Federation Colors," which closely approximates the historical development. Germany's national flag, known today throughout the world, had its origins in the wars of liberation against Napoleon (1813), and in particular with the uniforms of Lützow's Volunteer Corps. Most of the members of this unit were students who joined together to oppose the French occupation of Germany. The volunteers came from all of the small German states and were led by the Prussian major Adolf von Lützow. Since the fighters initially wore a variety of uniforms and civilian clothing, they were soon supplied with uniforms of various colors which were dyed black, with brass buttons (having the appearance of gold) and red lapels. These colors also symbolize the flag of the Holy Roman Empire of the German Nation.

Seven Volunteer Corps Students Choose the Colors

In June 1815, seven Volunteer Corps students who were active after the war with various Corps members in Jena combined with other national- and republican-minded students to found the first student fraternity, choose the colors black-red-gold. On the fourth anniversary (October 18, 1817) of the Battle of Leipzig, around 500 fraternity members and a few professors from the black-red-gold German states gathered at the Wartburg to demand freedom and a unified state. In May of 1832, 30,000 participants demonstrated for national and democratic goals at the Hambach Fest, carrying with them for the first time a black-red-gold flag. The inscription in the central red section, "Germany's rebirth," made their goal clear: the establishment of a German national state.

The democratic revolutionaries of 1848 called the flag "Tri-Color," borrowing from the term used by the French for their flag. This combination of colors was supported by a statement from the wars of liberation: Out of the blackness of bondage, through bloody battles, to the golden light of freedom. On November 13 the national flag was officially proclaimed in the state law gazette, after having been agreed upon by the German National Assembly in Frankfurt am Main.

Black-red-gold ultimately became the national colors of the flag of the German Empire from 1871 until 1918 and of the Weimar Republic (1919-1933), although its adoption at that time led to quarrels. The Nazis subsequently introduced the swastika flag, which, along with the imperial black-red-gold, became the national flag.

1848-1857 – Waves of Emigrants to North America

From the 17th century on, German immigrants had established themselves in many parts of America, having left their native land for economic, political, or religious reasons. The failure of the German revolution of 1848 brought with it a veritable wave of emigration, for the most part occasioned by political repression.[3] By 1857, this exodus had reached its peak. The great majority of these emigrants were former revolutionaries, who henceforth were known as Forty-Eighters, a term that is still used today. (Cf. Appendix 3, p. 87.)

The exodus of German democrats in the second half of the 19th century is tragically significant. What would have happened if the "Forty-Eighters" had been able to stay in their German homelands? It is highly probable that, due to the democratic, liberal, and freedom-loving orientation of those politicians and intellectuals who emigrated, the extreme conservatism and nationalism of the pre-and-post-World-War-I German Empire would not have developed. The logical result: perhaps we would have been spared both world wars, to say nothing of Hitler!

Berlin, March 18th 1848. Democratic 48er revolutionaries defeat the Prussian Army.

---

3. The German historian Dr. Joachim Reppmann is an authoritative researcher on German emigration. Since 1978, "Yogi" Reppmann has concentrated on North German emigration to the United States. In this connection he initiated the founding of the American/Schleswig-Holstein Heritage Society (ASHHS); he as well as other historians continue to bring new material to light. Joachim Reppmann had the main responsibility for setting this Holocaust project in motion.

The Emigration of Forty-Eighters

From 1851 on the second wave of emigration follows, conditioned by the defeat of the Schleswig-Holstein rebels. In addition to the politically active Forty-Eighters[4], many farmers and laborers now leave their German homeland along with their families. Young single men leave as well, to avoid the military conscription that has been in effect since 1867 in the Prussian province of Schleswig-Holstein.

These North German "pioneers" write thousands of letters to the homeland they have left behind, praising in brilliant colors their new life in the North American states. Their correspondence circulates back home, and newspapers also print excerpts from their letters. In this way "emigration fever" grips more and more people.[5]

The Emigrations Reach their Peak

Nineteenth-century emigrations reach their peak between 1865 and 1875 and from 1880 to 1885. After this, emigration from Germany and other European countries becomes less significant. Especially during the American Civil War (1861-1865), the influx of German immigrants comes almost to a standstill.

According to reliable estimates, from 1821 to 1912 almost 5.5 million German-speaking Europeans emigrated to the United States. The areas of German settlement are the Middle West, Texas, Kentucky, Maryland, New Jersey, Oregon, and Washington. By preference, Germans settled in regions with agricultural specialities such as the Corn Belt (Ohio, Iowa) and the Wheat Belt (Kansas, North Dakota), and in dairy farming regions (Wisconsin and New York).

---

4. Many of the German Forty-Eighters emigrated to the United States, including a large contingent from northern Germany. These energetic and talented individuals provided what amounted to an intellectual transfusion in the various Midwestern locales where they settled.

It was to this "heartland", not to escape from poverty, as is sometimes assumed, but to seek freedom from repression following the failed democratic revolution of 1848. They had only one goal in mind: freedom and self-determination. These basic principles, including responsibility for oneself and for the community, have always characterized the American way of thinking.

Please have a look at the moving educational video "Forty-Eighters and Friends," YouTube or: www.Moin-Moin.us (Menu 'Videos-English')

5. A striking parallel: since 2014, millions of war refugees from Arab countries as well as economically motivated asylum seekers have been fleeing to western Europe—in this case motivated not by letters, but by modern means of communication.

1840 – Anti-Semitism in the 19th Century

With the beginning of the 19th century, the Anti-Semitism[6] that was always latently present intensifies in Europe. The hostility toward Jews is closely related to the burgeoning of nationalism beginning in 1840. Anti-Semitism develops with particular intensity in the politics and culture of Germany and Austria. During the "March revolution" of 1848-49, especially in the southern and eastern German regions, severe anti-Jewish excesses take place. The image created is of Jews as the perpetrators of all evils. Both rebellious farmers and, at the opposite extreme, anti-revolutionary citizens, threaten to annihilate the Jews, who are blamed for economic distress on the one hand and for the revolution on the other. Thus it becomes clear: the Nazi persecution of the Jewish population in the 20th century, ultimately leading to mass murder (Holocaust), has its roots in the mid-19th century.

1871 – The Founding of the German Empire

There is debate among historians concerning the extent to which the events of 1848-49 influenced the founding of a unified German state. In any case, the foundation of the German Empire took place during the German-French War of 1870-71. The victories over the French armies in August and September 1870 made it possible to transform the alliance between the North German Confederation that had existed since 1866 and the South German states into a national German-language union whose people spoke a variety of dialects. The new federal state became the new German Empire.

Wilhelm Friedrich Ludwig, King of Prussia and first German Emperor (22 March 1797 – 9 March 1888)

Otto Eduard Leopold, Prince of Bismarck, Duke of Lauenburg (1 April 1815 – 30 July 1898)

---

6. Anti-Semitism extends as a central theme throughout history, reaching its most horrific expression during the Nazi regime; now, however, in the 21st century, it has again become evident in renewed hostility to Jews in many parts of the world.

The Proclamation of Wilhelm I

This German Empire - also known as the Second German Empire, after the Holy Roman Empire of the German Nation - was composed of four kingdoms, six grand duchies, five duchies, eight principalities, as well as the Hansa Cities of Hamburg, Lübeck, and Bremen. Foundation Day was January 18, 1871[7], with the proclamation of Wilhelm I in the Palace of Versailles, followed by parliamentary elections in March and the new constitution in April 1871. On May 4, 1871, the constitution came into force, retroactive to January 1. The new empire in the center of Europe was a federal state, a constitutional state, an empire, the state of Prussian hegemony, a military state, and above all a German national state.

Otto von Bismarck - the First Chancellor of the German Empire

Otto Eduard Leopold von Bismarck-Schönhausen (1815-1898) was one of the most important and authoritative politicians and statesmen of the 19th century in Germany. As a member of the nobility, Otto von Bismarck first made a name for himself in conservative circles by representing the interests of the Junkers (landowners). From 1862 on, with a short break in 1873, he served as prime minister and foreign minister of Prussia. In the German-Danish War (1864) and the German War (1866), he established the political supremacy of Prussia in Germany. Bismarck was the first chancellor of the German Empire and remained in office from 1871 to 1890; in this capacity he was the driving force behind the resolution of the "German question" in favor of federalism. In foreign policy, he was in favor of a European balance of power. Because of the forcefulness of his approach in determining the politics of the newly established empire, he has gone down in history as the "iron chancellor."

From 1871 on, the Reichstag (parliament) was the body through which, for the first time, the parties were able to exert political influence. Although they had a say in determining legislation, the government was of course appointed by the Kaiser. The role of the Reichstag was also limited by federalism, by the predominance of Prussia in the Bundesrat (the representation of the individual German states), by limitations in the budget laws, and by decisions concerning the military.

For the most part, the parties of the 1860s continued to exist in the empire. The socialists, unified in 1875, assumed the name Social Democratic Party of Germany (SPD) in 1891. The leftist liberals were spread out over various parties. In 1876 the more traditional conservatives formed a party in all areas of the realm. In spite of their name, the German Conservative Party, they were predominantly a Prussian party and for that reason gave priority to representing Prussian interests and those of the land owners and the upper echelon of officers. Of the 74 Reichstag representatives in 1887, 53 (70 percent!) were aristocrats, who supported the empire but sought to maintain the autonomy of monarchical Prussia. In 1878 a new party was founded, the Christian Socialist Workers Party (known as the Christian Socialist Party from 1881 on). This was the first party to officially adopt anti-Semitism in its program.

---

7. The anniversary of the coronation in 1701 of Elector Friedrich III of Brandenburg as Friedrich I, the first king of Prussia. The Hall of Mirrors in the Palace of Versailles, with its ceiling painting celebrating Louis XIV as the conqueror of German cities and lands, was chosen for Wilhelm's proclamation as a way of emphasizing the dramatic shift in the European balance of powers. This insulting choice cemented German-French enmity for decades to come.

Heinrich Mann

The protagonist of "The Underling" is Diederich Hessling, an example of a certain type of person in the society of the empire. A slave to the authorities, cowardly and lacking in civil courage, a fellow traveler and conformist, Hessling identifies with the ambitions to world power of the radical nationalists who long for the coming (First) World War. As a critical and symbolic contrast, Heinrich Mann has the 1848 revolutionary Buck, a friend of Hessling's father who represents the atrophy of liberalism, die under the very eyes of the protagonist.

1871 to 1914 – The Citizen as "Underling"

With Article 3 of the imperial constitution, definitively dictated by Bismarck, the "members (underlings, citizens) of each federal state" are made subordinate to a single national German citizenship. The term "underling," now officially established in the constitution, becomes the symbol of moral cowardice, obedience, devotion, fulfillment of commands, and conformity. These are typical qualities of most citizens in the era of "Wilhelmism." The masses—supposedly under the protection of democratic laws—are now of use only to the authorities and the military. It is this fundamental character imprint that leads the populace into the First World War and later prepares the ground for the National Socialists.[8]

Thus the constitution of the German Empire had introduced through the "back door" a special form of absolutism again, such as had existed in previous centuries as the authority of the state. The civic term "subject," which turns the members of the lower classes into underlings and consciously devalues them, had been transformed after the French Revolution into "free citizen," a term that had had currency in the German lands as well. Now the free citizen is once again restricted, becoming in the German Empire the underling who has as little as possible to say and is permitted to say nothing.

Heinrich Mann (born in Lübeck in 1871, died in Santa Monica, California in 1950), the older brother of Thomas Mann, was one of the few German writers who dared to analyze in his works the authoritarian structures of the German Empire in the period of Wilhelmism. He did this in three novels known today as the Empire Trilogy, the first part of which ("The Underling") is the most convincing. The novel was not published until 1919, shortly after the end of WWI.

---

8. The 2011 German film "Lessons of a Dream" gives a rough approximation of the societal situation and the social opposites of the untra-nationalistic Wilhelminian period. The film concerns the German English teacher Konrad Koch, who introduced soccer to Germany in 1874.

1879 – Anti-Semitism Becomes "Socially Acceptable"

The protestant minister Adolf Stoecker and his Christian-Socialist Party make hostility to Jews acceptable on all levels of society. This party and others with an anti-Semitic orientation gain seats in the Reichstag. Decades before Hitler's seizure of power, a further foundation stone for the racist ideology of National Socialism and for mass murder is laid in written references to the "annihilation of the Jewish people," even involving an indirect connection with transportation by railroad (!)[9]

A bad omen, since 1899 was also the year in which the boxcar you see in Fagen Museum was built. Railroad cars like this one were manufactured in several German cities at that time because of the need for transporting people and goods by means of the steadily growing network of railroads. The manufacturers of locomotives, streetcars, passenger cars, and freight cars were located, for example, in Gotha, Bautzen, Görlitz, Dessau, Bremen, and Halle.

Along with the submissiveness of the masses and their constant cheering for the Kaiser, anti-Semitism becomes established in the German Empire as virtually socially acceptable. The same is true of Austria. In his novels and stories, the Austrian Jewish writer and doctor Arthur Schnitzler (1862-1931) deals in depth with the hostility encountered by his Jewish fellow citizens everywhere in the society of the Austro-Hungarian monarchy. Jewish students suffer under the Waidhofen Resolution, an anti-Semitic principle adopted by various dueling fraternities in 1896.[10]

Criticism of Jews, and insults to them and their institutions, becomes more or less normal. Thus the year 1879 is considered the year of the birth of "modern" anti-Semitism, in which nationalistic, anti-liberal, anti-capitalistic, and racist motives are interconnected. Thus a conglomeration of constant baiting of Jewish fellow citizens develops from many sides. The anti-Semitic German People's Party (DVP), whose delegates demand the deportation of the Jews, becomes established in parliament. As early as 1917, the party organ of the DVP displays the swastika.

---

9. The German Socialist Party, for example, demands in its program of 1899: "It is the duty of the anti-Semitic party to heighten knowledge of the true essence of the Jewish people […]. Given the development of modern means of transportation, the Jewish question could become a global matter in the course of the 20th century and as such be definitively resolved in consort with other peoples of the world by means of complete separation and (if self-defense requires it) the final annihilation of the Jewish people."

10. Anti-Semitism intensified in 19th-century Germany and Austria among students who were members of dueling fraternities. For their part, Jewish students reacted by founding their own Jewish fraternities, which accepted as a principle that any anti-Semitic expression made by a student was to be answered with a challenge to a duel. This gave some Jewish fraternities the reputation of being especially aggressive, and led to prohibitions. Toward the end of the 19th century, many pistol duels resulting in deaths were reported. The successes of Jewish fraternity students in dueling and fencing soon created an embarrassing situation, since they contradicted the alleged notion of Jews as cowardly or jittery during duels. The initial reaction to this took place in Austria, where the student dueling organizations seized on the Waidhofen Resolutions, alleging that all Jews were without honor and therefore not permitted to duel. This tactic was applied in Germany as well, although not until after the First World War: "Jews are devoid of honor and may therefore not participate in duels, no matter what the weapon."

1914 to 1918 – The First World War

The First World War was waged in Europe, the Near East, Africa, East Asia, and on the oceans of the world, claiming approximately 17 million lives. The starting point was July 28, 1914, with Austria-Hungary's declaration of war on Serbia. This was preceded by the assassination in Sarajevo (June 28, 1914) and the "July Crisis" it triggered. The major participants and alliances on the one side were Germany, Austria-Hungary, the Ottoman Empire, and Bulgaria, and on the other France, Great Britain and the British Empire, Russia, Serbia, Belgium, Italy, Rumania, Japan, and the United States. A total of 40 countries took part in the most extensive war in history up to that time. Approximately 70 million soldiers were in arms. The war ended on November 11, 1918 with the victory of the coalition of the Triple Entente.[11]

At the beginning of the war, Europeans display a broad spectrum of reactions from protest and an attitude of denial, through helplessness and shock, to (especially in Germany) patriotic exuberance and even hysteria. In general, though, there is no general enthusiasm for war, it is only military propaganda that portrays it as such. The proletarian and peasant strata stand almost as a block in opposition. Large parts of the middle-class and academic strata, however, welcome the impending event; for example, the conservative middle class reacts to Austria-Hungary's ultimatum and declaration of war against Serbia with patriotic parades, such as the one on July 25, 1914 in Berlin, with as many as 30,000 participants.

In the smaller cities and in the country, by contrast, the prevailing mood is distinctly depressed, reflective, and pessimistic. The threat of war brings out similarly restrained and dejected reactions among the working class of the industrial centers, but the broad masses of people tend to simply accept what is happening. Nonetheless, in Germany as well as in Great Britain and France, several series of demonstrations against the surge toward war take place at the end of July 1914; there are 288 meetings and marches in approximately 160 German cities, including a group of more than 100,000 in central Berlin despite its having been banned by the municipal authorities. But the anti-war attitude in Germany suddenly turns, as news arrives of the Russian partial mobilization on July 28, 1914. Now the Social Democrats, like the worker movements of other countries, join the unified political front. Only a few days before this the Social Democrats had come out against the "warmongering" of their own government.

On August 1, 1914, almost 50,000 gather before the Berlin city palace for the second speech of Wilhelm II, who announces from the balcony that he no longer knows "any [individual] parties or religious denominations." Three days later, on August 4, he adds to this: "I know only Germans." Chancellor Bethmann Hollweg then cleverly portrays Russia as the supposed aggressor. SPD party chairman Hugo Haase, who had organized numerous anti-war demonstrations and had fought within the party until August 3 against the acceptance of war credits, declares on behalf of the SPD on the following day: "We will not abandon our own country in the hour of danger." In each of the belligerent countries a broad political solidarity now develops, along with a concerned, but serious-minded and determined acceptance of the war.

---

11. The term Triple Entente refers to the military coalition (United Kingdom, France, and Russia) in the First World War that was opposed to the Central Powers (main allies: the German Empire and the Habsburg Monarchy of Austria-Hungary). The military alliance of the Triple Entente was based on the Pact of London from September 5, 1914, concluded one month before the outbreak of war. Its foreign policy stance before entering the war was as a defensive coalition. It was important for the United States (declaration of war on April 6, 1917) to be seen only as an associated power.

> # The Story of Another Famous Railroad Car!
>
> The city and region of Compiègne, 80 kilometers north of Paris, are known for the signing of two armistice agreements between Germany and France. From April 1917 to March 1918, the city housed the main headquarters of the French army. On November 11, 1918, in a dining car that had been turned into an office for Marshal Ferdinand Foch, the Supreme Allied Commander, the peace treaty that ended the First World War was concluded. The car was subsequently placed in a museum in Paris and then brought back for display to Compiègne.
>
> Twenty-two years later, on June 22, 1940, a second armistice was concluded, this time for the surrender of France to Nazi Germany. On this occasion, Hitler had the car brought back to the very spot where the earlier armistice had been signed. Afterwards it was taken to Berlin for a week-long display. In the course of the war it was brought to various locations, ending up in Crawinkel in Thuringia. There, in March 1945, it was destroyed by German soldiers at the advance of American troops.

Railroads as Wartime Transportation

The wheels of Europe's railroads begin to roll; in passenger cars and especially in freight cars hundreds of thousands of soldiers are taken to the front. In Germany freight cars are quickly adapted, with 24 bunks each for lying and sitting. In his impressive autobiography "A Youth in Germany," the leftist politician and writer Ernst Toller describes his journey in a freight car from Switzerland to Germany: "Each car has a sign: for sixteen men or eight horses; unfinished boards smelling of resin serve as benches . . . At the stations people give us cards with the picture of the Kaiser and the words: "I no longer know any parties."

The devastations of World War I were enormous. From February to the middle of December 1916, one of the most cataclysmic battles ever known, and the first to use weaponry on a grand scale, took place in Verdun in eastern France. In the constant barrages of the "Hell of Verdun" more than 300,000 died—162,000 Frenchmen and 143,000 Germans. Later on, the German military instituted as its new naval strategy a policy of "submarine warfare without warning," thus provoking the United States to enter the war in 1917.

The American historian Richard J. Bessel estimates the number of soldiers in the German army in May 1918 at seven million, of whom just over four million saw action in the western front, 950,000 in the eastern front, and close to two million in the occupation armies of the conquered territories. In October 1918 the number of German soldiers in active service had already dropped to approximately six million. This means that within five months about one million German soldiers had either been killed in action, died of other causes, been wounded and were unfit to fight, had become sick (due, for example, to a wave of influenza), or had simply deserted.

Military propaganda portrays patriotic exuberance and even hysteria.

German Troop Morale

Following the horrible slaughter of the war and the spring offensive of 1918, the morale of the German troops had drastically diminished. Even months before the armistice, the army was in a state of dissolution. Toward the end of 1917, as many as ten percent of the troops used their transportation across Germany from the eastern to the western front (to a large extent in railroad freight cars!) as an opportunity for desertion. According to historian Bessel: "At the eastern front, the widespread war-weariness led to frequent instances of refusal to obey orders; in one case about 5,000 soldiers refused to be shunted to the western front, and in another there were bloody encounters between officers and enlisted men." The number of disciplinary offenses climbed rapidly.

In July 1918, General Ludendorff[12] lamented the "increasing number of unauthorized absences, instances of cowardice, and refusals to obey orders in the face of the enemy at the eastern front, along with the lenient judgments often granted to such criminal offenses at court-martials. The military authorities have been trying in vain to counter this dwindling of fighting spirit through more severe punishments."

Reports on the reception of the hundreds of thousands of German combatants and prisoners of war who returned home in 1918 differed greatly. The German officers' corps presented only

---

12. Erich Friedrich Wilhelm Ludendorff (1865-1937), a German general and politician, had as Quartermaster General and deputy of Paul von Hindenburg, the Chief of General Staff, decisive influence on the conduct of the war. He was responsible for the failed German spring offensive of 1918 and was one of the originators of the "Stab-in-the-back" legend described later. At the time of the Weimar Republic he was active in the right-wing national movement, took part in two unsuccessful attempts to take over the government (the Kapp putsch in 1920 and Hitler's beer hall putsch in 1923), and was a representative of the German People's Freedom Party in parliament.

images of "war veterans who, upon their return to Germany are humiliated by civilians who are not prepared to welcome returning soldiers with the honor they deserve." This estimation, however, had to do primarily with returning officers, and there is no indication of a general enmity towards war veterans. Historian Bessel points out that "contemporary reports on the reception of soldiers returning from the trenches often sound quite different. Numerous German civil and military authorities, as well as workers' councils and many employers, made sure that returning soldiers were given a festive welcome." Far from wanting to ignore or even to mock returning soldiers, the civilian population seemed to make the greatest efforts to show them gratitude and respect. The streets of most German cities and villages were decorated with flags and flowers as the soldiers returned from the front or made their way home from their barracks.

The Patriotism of German Jews

The patriotism of thousands of German soldiers of the Jewish faith who reported for duty at the front in the First World War is well-known. Ernst Toller was one of these. After fighting at Verdun and being decorated for bravery, he suffered a psychological and physical breakdown and began writing pacifist poetry. Lying in a military hospital, he commented: "At noon the doctor comes, a Jew; he examines me and says, all pacifists should be shot." Toller later adds: "In the admissions room sits a nationalistic Jewish sergeant, who growls that I should thank my Creator that the doctors even bother to look after me . . ."

In parliament, accusations were raised on the conservative side against "Jewish slackers." Apparently in order to clarify this, the Center Party representative Matthias Erzberger (1875-1921) demanded that the Chancellor should draw up and publish "a detailed table of the entire personnel of all military groupings . . . separated according to gender, age of compulsory service, income, religion." The conservatives, the national liberals, the Center Party, as well as a few SPD-representatives agreed to this proposal. The majority of the SPD and the leftist Liberals rejected it, since a categorization according to religious criteria was in contradiction to the principles of a state governed by law and order. It is not clear whether Erzberger already knew at this time of the internal edict issued by the Minister of War for a so-called Jewish census and wanted to supplement it, or did not yet know of the planned army count. The results of this statistical inquiry of November 1, 1917, were kept quiet until 1919, because it showed that approximately as many Jewish as Christian soldiers were in the service (approximately ten percent as volunteers), and that the number of war dead was correspondingly similar.

As director of the armistice commission, Erzberger had the thankless task of signing the armistice agreement on November 11, 1918 in the Forest of Compiègne, thereby arousing the enmity of all those, including people like Adolf Hitler and his brown-shirted comrades, who could not get over losing the war. As finance minister of the newly established Weimar Republic he raised taxes in 1919 in order to restore the country's financial stability, and thus increasingly became a target of inflammatory right-wing propaganda. After surviving an assassination attempt in 1920, he was murdered by two right-wing former naval officers in 1921 while on convalescent leave in the Black Forest. The assassins fled the country and were granted amnesty by the Nazis when they returned in 1933.

Loyalty Did Not Help Them Later

The loyalty to Germany of Jews who had fought in the war did not help them later or to escape Nazi persecution. Shortly after the war, the Dolchstoßlegende (myth of a stab in the back) was fabricated by right-wing groups and the military, who claimed that Germany had not lost the war in the field, but had been betrayed by the actions of left-wing groups at home. Anti-Semitic politicians and organizations linked these purported actions with a false image of "international Jewry," thus supplying the burgeoning Nazi movement with material for its racist policies.

Stab in the Back Myth

An illustration from a 1919 Austrian postcard showing a caricatured Jew stabbing the German Army in the back with a dagger. The capitulation was blamed upon the unpatriotic populace, the Socialists, Bolsheviks, the Weimar Republic, and especially the Jews.

When the Nazis came to power in 1933, they made the legend an integral part of their official history of the 1920s, portraying the Weimar Republic as the work of the "November criminals" who used the stab in the back to seize power while betraying the nation. The Nazi propaganda depicted Weimar Republic as "a morass of corruption, degeneracy, national humiliation, ruthless persecution of the honest 'national opposition'—fourteen years of rule by Jews, Marxists, and 'cultural Bolsheviks', who had at last been swept away by the National Socialist movement under Adolf Hitler and the victory of the 'national revolution' of 1933".

1919 to 1933 – The Weimar Republic

The Weimar Republic came into being in the wake of the German revolution of 1918 and 1919, instigated by leftist forces following the excesses of the conservative powers that supported the continuation of the war. The Republic received its name from the city in Thuringia where the German National Assembly held its initial meetings and ratified its constitution, which went into force on August 14, 1919 and established Germany as a federal republic. The Assembly elected the Social Democrat Friedrich Ebert (1871-1925) president and Philipp Scheidemann chancellor. In its day, the Weimar constitution was considered progressive. After the March revolution of 1848, it represents the second attempt, and the first successful one, at establishing a liberal democracy in Germany.

The history of the Weimar Republic can be divided into three segments. In the years of crisis from 1919 to 1923, Germany had to struggle with the aftermath of the war — hyperinflation, numerous coup attempts, and political murders. From 1924 to 1929, it experienced a period of relative stability, economic recovery, and recognition and esteem by other countries. The world economic crisis beginning at the end of 1929, government by presidential decree after the collapse of the Grand Coalition in March 1930, and the rise of National Socialism, finally brought about its demise.

The "Stab in the Back" Myth and Difficult Beginnings

The young republic inherited several structural problems from the days of the empire, such as the economic and social systems and denominationally-based educational policies. There were as well other phenomena that directly influenced the failure of the Weimar democracy, such as the fact that large parts of the population rejected the notions of bourgeois democracy and republic. Citing the notorious stab-in-the-back legend, conservatives and right-wing extremists blamed the new democratic government for the loss of the war and the humiliating Versailles peace treaty. And on the side of the left, the fighting during the November revolution resulted in irreconcilable differences between the Communists and the Social Democrats. This prevented them from proceeding in common cause against the enemies of the Republic, which in turn favored the rise of the Nazis.

After the death of Friedrich Ebert in 1925, the presidency went to Paul von Hindenburg, whose view of the republican form of government was emphatically critical. At times, as many as 17 parties were represented in parliament, and there were 20 changes of cabinet in 14 years. Eleven minority cabinets were dependent on the toleration of parties that had no part in a government coalition.

The overall economic conditions, after a relative strengthening of the Republic following the great inflation of 1923-24, contributed to destabilization. Especially in Germany, social and economic turmoil resulted from the 1929 "Black Friday" of the New York Stock Exchange. The withdrawal of short-term credits by American investors, which had fed a temporary stimulus, contributed considerably to the economic depression: faltering sales of goods, declining production, massive layoffs and unemployment, along with diminishing purchasing power brought about a downward spiral on a previously unknown scale. The systems of social safeguards, still in the process of development, were not equal to these problems.

1933 to 1945 – The Nazi Dictatorship of the Third Reich

There is scarcely a historian who, in retrospect, is surprised at what now took place. Since as of March 1930 there no longer was a government controlled by a majority in parliament, President Hindenburg and the chancellor appointed by him governed for the most part with the aid of emergency decrees. The parliamentary elections in 1930 resulted in the rise of the radical rightist National Socialist German Workers Party (NSDAP) that had been founded in 1920. It became a significant force in the Weimar party spectrum. Along with it, the "solution to the Jewish question," conceived during the Empire by anti-Semitic politicians, remained an important element of Nazi propaganda in the Weimar period.

Hitler as "Führer" of the National Socialists

With the conservative DNVP (German National Peoples Party) and other rightist organizations, a new constellation of power forms at the beginning of 1933 around Adolf Hitler as the leader of the Nazi party. On January 30, Hitler is appointed Chancellor. As the absolute "Führer" of the National Socialists, it does not take him long to destroy the democratic, law-and-order, and federal structures of the Republic and to establish his dictatorship.[13]

---

13. The Austrian writer of Jewish background Stefan Zweig (1881-1942) describes the Nazis' murderous strategy in his biography "The World of Yesterday," which first appeared posthumously in Sweden in 1942: " . . . National Socialism, with its perfidiously deceptive techniques, was careful to hide the radicality of its goals until the world had become hardened. Thus they carried out their methods carefully: always one dose at a time, and after each dose a brief pause . . . and since the European conscience . . . most zealously emphasized its indifference—since these violent deeds were taking place beyond their borders—the doses became stronger and stronger, until finally they destroyed all of Europe. Hitler achieved nothing more brilliant than this tactic of a slow sounding-out of the situation and gradual intensification in the face of a Europe that was becoming morally and soon also militarily weaker and weaker . . ."

The National Socialist party had around 850,000 members at the beginning of 1933; in the following years this number grew to 5.3 million in 1939 and, finally, 7.7 million in May 1943. The Munich headquarters was under the control of Rudolf Hess until it was made answerable to Hitler in May 1941 and, with the new designation of "party chancellery," directed by the long-standing chief of staff Martin Bormann. The party had 18 sub-organizations, including the League of German Girls (BDM), the Hitler Youth (HJ), as well as the notorious military alliances known as the "Protective Detachment" (General SS and Armed SS) and the "Storm Division" (SA). The Nazi central file index (50 tons of cards), following the prevention of its planned destruction in 1945, was taken to the Berlin Document Center for safekeeping.

1933 – With the Blessing of the Churches

The national extremists on the right bring about another fateful shift on March 21, 1933. On the so-called "day of Potsdam," Hitler and von Hindenburg seal the bond between their National Socialist and German National parties in Potsdam's legendary Garrison Church. From this point on, their ultimately destructive alignment works in concert.

The Garrison Church, the 200-year-old resting place of Prussian kings, was viewed even before Hitler's rise as a stronghold of rightist views. Even during the Weimar period this Protestant church was a pilgrimage site for anti-democrats. From March 21, 1933 on, it becomes a sacred place for the Nazis, with the blessing of authoritative representatives of the Nazi-guided Organization of German Christians, whose actions are based on racism and anti-Semitism. Its overseers are state-appointed church committees and state commissioners. The Garrison community includes the Potsdam Nazi pastors Curt Koblanck, Werner Schütz, Rudolf Damrath, and Johannes Doehring. The latter's father, the Berlin Cathedral pastor Bruno Doehring, had issued the call for a "Holy War" in 1914.

In the church elections of July 1933, the Nazi-directed German Church along with the Nazi-influenced group "Gospel and Church," received a two-thirds majority in the church councils. Only a smaller portion of Protestants remain loyal to their Confessing Church (BK). This is an opposition movement opposing attempts at a "bringing into line" of the precepts and organization of the German Evangelical Church (DEK) in the period of National Socialism. One of the most prominent representative of the Confessing Church is Dietrich Bonhoeffer (cf. the subsequent section "Resistance and Rescue of Jewish Fellow Citizens", p. 48).

On August 19, 1933, almost 3,000 Nazi party members meet in the Garrison Church for a heroic consecration of the flag. Additional large events put on by Nazi organizations form the "program" of the church. On September 3, 1939, a full-house religious service is held at which soldiers leaving for the front are blessed. The victory over Poland is celebrated in Potsdam from October 4th through 10th by the daily ringing of bells. Even on January 24, 1945 the Nazis carry out a so-called church celebration to motivate those army and SS units who are still fighting on to final victory. But the liberators are drawing ever closer. On April 14, 1945 British bombers destroy this symbol of Nazi believers. Matthias Grünzig ("The Demon of Potsdam," *Die Zeit*, March 31, 2016) writes: "The building in which, from the time it was constructed, war was sanctified, itself fell victim to war."

1933 – Books Burn in German Cities

Heinrich Heine's prophecy more than 100 years earlier about the banning and destruction of freedom-loving art and culture is fully carried out by the Nazis immediately after their assumption of power. The public book burnings in Germany, with emphasis on May 10, 1933, are planned and carried out by the Nazi-oriented German Student Union, with professors and members of Nazi party organizations also participating. Works by outlawed authors and scientists are thrown into blazing fires on the former Berlin Opera Square and in almost 80 German university cities and others both large and small. The book burnings are high points of the "Campaign against the non-German spirit" organized by the general staff and are the beginnings of the systematic persecution of Jewish, Marxist, and other writers disagreeable to the Nazis.

Book burnings date back to the practice of the Roman Catholic Church beginning in the 4th century and had their high point during the Inquisition. Here, too, it was only books that were burned at first, but later on this led to the burning of human beings as well (cf. Heinrich Heine). The book burnings were usually public and were the result of moral, political, or religious objections to the content of the writings. There were dozens of book burnings from the 15th century to the modern period, in the United States as well, with the country's entrance into the First World War in 1917. In many states of the union at that time, books—especially German-language textbooks—were taken indiscriminately from library shelves to the accompaniment of patriotic songs. Such events were organized by school administrations, as was the case in Davenport, Iowa.

The student organizations keep to their strictly ordered plan for the funeral pyre on the evening of May 10, partly because it is being broadcast as a series of reports by Deutsche Welle (German radio). The public reading of "fire sayings" is also obligatory. In all the cities, university professors and others give speeches as the previously confiscated books—in Berlin alone around 25,000, and untold thousands elsewhere—are destroyed by fire. In Berlin propaganda minister Joseph Goebbels gives the event official sanction through his own "fiery" speech, in the truest sense of the word. In the pouring rain and accompanied by the sounds of an SA brass band, a parade of torches precedes this abstruse happening. The head of a broken bust of the Jewish doctor and sex researcher Magnus Hirschfeld is carried aloft at the end of a pole. Bordered by 70,000 curious onlookers, the parade marches through the Brandenburg Gate to the Opera Square (the Bebel Square of today) with the fraternity students in their ornate outfits, professors in their gowns, units of the SA and SS and the Hitler Youth, all escorted by police on horseback. The square is lit up by the spotlights of the weekly news reporters. Since the funeral pyre cannot be set on fire because of the driving rain, the fire department helps out with canisters of gas; all together, the books of 94 authors are burned. The singing of the Horst Wessel Song ends the event, which is broadcast live by German radio.

At the same time book burnings are carried out in the university cities of Bonn, Braunschweig, Bremen, Breslau, Dortmund, Dresden, Frankfurt am Main, Göttingen, Greifswald, Hannover, Hannoversch Münden, Kiel, Königsberg, Landau, Marburg, Munich, Münster, Nuremberg, Rostock, Worms, and Würzburg. Previously, on May 8, books had already been thrown into the flames in the university city of Gießen.

The "Combat Alliance for German Culture" in Flensburg

A good two months before this, however, Flensburg, one of the north German Nazi strongholds, demonstrates its early loyalty with a book burning on March 20, at which Hitler Youth members occupy the municipal youth center at the Norder Gate, gather up brochures and books that in their opinion do not represent National Socialism and burn them on the spot at Norder Gate Square. This was not the only book burning in Flensburg, although there was no university in this city and therefore no organized student groups. Instead, the "Combat Alliance for German Culture" appropriates the literature it finds hateful and sets up a book burning at the central parade ground for May 30. The official "fire speech" is given by the actor Ferdinand Schröder, who is also the director and chairman of the Combat Alliance. The books, most of which are collected from libraries, burn for three hours.

Because of the heavy rain in many locales on May 10, the actual book-burning day, the operation is postponed, occasioning the staging of eight additional book burnings between then and May 19, in Erlangen, Halle an der Saale, Hamburg, Heidelberg, Cologne, Mannheim, and Kassel. In Darmstadt the burning does not take place until June 21, and in Freiburg there is a postponement until June 24, the day of the Nazi midsummer celebration. On this occasion the newly-appointed chancellor of Freiburg University, the philosopher Martin Heidegger, gives a speech: "... o Flame, proclaim to us, shine your light and show us the way from which there is no turning back! Ignite, you flames, catch fire, you hearts!" The universities of Stuttgart, Tübingen, and Singen show some civil courage; the commissar of the student fraternities of Württemberg, Gerhard Schumann, forbids participation in the campaign, and maintains his ban in spite of the protests of several fraternities.

"Mein Kampf" Declared that Hitler had always been an Anti-Semite

The hostility toward Jews, bordering on lunacy, intensified rapidly after the beginning of the Nazi dictatorship, which called itself the "Third Reich." The term "Thousand-Year Reich" also was used in Nazi propaganda, in blasphemous reference to the Christian notion of the thousand-year rule of Jesus Christ following the defeat of Satan. In February 1920 Hitler had already demanded in his NSDAP party program that Jews be excluded from German citizenship and all public offices, and that special "foreigners' laws" be created for them; in his equally programmatic work "Mein Kampf" of 1925-26 he declared that he had always be an anti-Semite.[14]

2,000 Anti-Jewish Laws and Ordinances are Enacted

The logical consequence of this continuing ideological abuse is the beginning of the Nazi purge, soon after their rise to power, of all Jews from German society. Their immediate goal is to force as many Jewish citizens as possible to emigrate, to weaken them economically, and to make social outcasts of them. This happens initially by means of SA terror, from 1934 on through the SS, and through state measures such as the "boycott of Jews" and a long list of laws. During the period of National Socialism, approximately 2,000 anti-Jewish laws and ordinances are enacted. The essentially legal basis that supports the increasingly extreme persecution of Jews are the "race laws" adopted by the Reichstag at the 7th Reich Party Day held in Nuremberg in 1935.

With the "Joining" of Austria in March 1938 the Nazi regime intensifies its anti-Jewish measures. Their goal now is expropriation ("Aryanization") across the entire Reich. Following a wave of terror by Austrian National Socialists, the "Jewish consultant" Adolf Eichmann establishes the "Central Agency for Jewish Emigration in Vienna." Parallel to their preparations for war, National Socialist representatives plan the hostage-taking, arrests, and murders of German and Austrian Jews.

---

14. The overthrown monarch Wilhelm II, living in exile in Holland since 1919, also supported the persecution of the Jews by the extreme right. In a letter to General Field Marshal August von Mackensen he topped off his own hatred of the Jews, writing about the "tribe of Judah" that had enjoyed a guest's privileges in Germany and, referring to the loss of the war, misused them: "No German should ever forget this, nor rest, until these parasites are eradicated from German soil and wiped out—this poisonous mushroom on the German oak!"

1938 – The Night of the Pogroms, November 9

The anti-Jewish infection of large parts of the population by the Nazis leads in the night of the 9th/10th November 1938 to the first nationwide incident in Germany, which the SA stirs up and the German police allows to happen. The November pogroms throughout the entire Reich have devastating consequences. Around 400 Jews are murdered or driven to suicide. More than 1,400 synagogues are set on fire, along with prayer rooms and other meeting spaces; thousands of shops, dwellings, and Jewish cemeteries are destroyed. Due to the breaking of the window-panes of synagogues, shops, and houses resulting from the destructive mania, the colloquial and trivializing Nazi expression "Reich Crystal Night" develops and is sometimes used even in recent historical works without further comment.

With the Nuremberg Laws, also known as the Nuremberg Race Laws or Aryan Laws, the National Socialists institutionalize their anti-Semitic ideology. The laws were unanimously passed by the Reichstag, which had been convened in Nuremberg solely for this purpose. They included the Law for the Protection of German Blood and German Honor—the so-called Blood Protection Law—and the Reich Citizens Law. Along with these two "racial laws," the Reich Flag Law also belongs to the collective term "Nuremberg Laws," although at the time it was not considered part of them. All three laws were announced in the Reich Law Gazette of September 16, 1935, with the notation "at the Reich Party Day of Freedom." They were abolished by the Allied Control Council Law No. 1 of September 20, 1945.

Following the pogroms, Reich Marshal Göring threatens on November 12, 1938: "If the German Reich should become involved in foreign conflicts, it is of course obvious that we in Germany will first and foremost think of carrying out a day of reckoning against the Jews." And on November 24, 1938, the following statement appears in the SS journal "The Black Corps": "The program is clear: complete removal, total separation! This would result in the actual and final end of Jewry in Germany, its total annihilation."

The Arrests Begin

Shortly before this, on November 10, the first mass arrests of people of the Jewish faith begins: the first 30,000 Jews are taken away to concentration camps in the following months.[15] Hundreds are murdered or die because of the prison conditions. Thus the pogroms mark the transition from the discrimination of German Jews to their systematic persecution and forced oppression, which by 1941 at the latest results in total Holocaust.

With the anti-Jewish laws and ordinances, among them the "Jews' penance," the victims of the November pogroms now must finance the rearmament of the perpetrators. The state-imposed impoverishment of the Jews due to these payments makes their emigration considerably more difficult. Göring then establishes on January 24, 1939 in Berlin the Reich central office for Jewish emigration, with the goal of "furthering the emigration of Jews from Germany with all possible means."

---

15. On October 22, 1940—the Feast of Tabernacles, chosen intentionally by the Nazi planners—Jews from southwest Germany are deported to concentration camps. In one instance, SS men and police force the 300 Jewish citizens from the town of Gailingen on the Swiss border to the freight station in Konstanz. Here transport trains with the notorious boxcars are waiting. Thousands of Jews in other cities and villages in Baden, the Palatinate, and the Saarland suffer the same horrible fate on this day. They are the first victims of the mass deportations and the Holocaust. (Source: *Die Zeit*, No. 42/2015, p. 19.)

1941 to 1945 – The Holocaust / Shoah

"The final solution of the Jewish question": as of July 1941, this is how the Nazis describe their goal of murdering all those they define as Jews in Europe and beyond. The term "final solution"—instead of annihilation or murder—is meant to disguise the Holocaust or Shoahh to the outside world, and to justify it ideologically within Germany. In earlier times, the term had been used to mean an organized expulsion or resettlement, such as had been insisted upon by German anti-Semites beginning about 1880. Hitler, however, in a speech in 1920, already talks of "eradicating the Jews root and branch."

On January 30, 1939, eight months before the German attack on Poland that began the Second World War, Hitler announces in the Reichstag the annihilation of the Jews. He speaks of the scant willingness of the democratic countries to take in persecuted Jews. He makes the following literal threat: "If international financial Jewry should be successful in plunging the nations into a world war once again, the result will be the annihilation of the Jewish race in Europe." Even before this Hitler had told the Czech foreign minister that the Jews would be "annihilated" if they could not be taken to some distant place. If the Anglo-Saxon countries did not cooperate in this process, they would have their deaths on their conscience.

The Nazis' plans from 1939 to 1941 for deporting the Jewish population from the German Reich and the conquered regions, and/or to resettle them as far away as Madagascar, are discarded for the most part because of their immense scope. The attack on Poland in itself brings 2.5 million Polish Jews into the German sphere of control and complicates the expulsion of German and Austrian Jews from the "Old Reich." By the end of 1939 some 200,000 Jews from eastern Europe are deported to the new eastern Polish governorship so that ethnic Germans can be resettled in eastern Poland. At the same time 90,000 Jews are driven over the border to Soviet-occupied eastern Poland.

The Deportations

The SS leadership develops numerous ideas for deporting Jewish people and imprisoning them in camps. The deportations and the establishment of ghettos, especially in occupied Poland (Warsaw, for example) along with the living conditions in the work camps results in innumerable fatalities by 1939-40. But there are even larger-scale SS mass murders; military squads murder 60,000 members of the Polish ruling class, including about 7,000 Jews, in order to prevent resistance to the German occupiers.

According to various documents, the Nazi planners consider the deportations and resettlements a gigantic task. Historians disagree as to how these plans should be assessed. The important German historian Hans Mommsen (1930-2015) takes the position that no systematic liquidation of European Jews had been considered until autumn of 1941; the colonization plans were certainly illusory, but had been meant seriously.

It is a little known fact that in an official decree of May 1943 the Nazis turned away from the term anti-Semitism. The reason was that they wanted to make distinctions between their new Arabian allies and the Jews. Being "anti-Semitic," after all, would also mean being against the Arabs, most of whom were also of Semitic origin.

1939 – The Railroad as Death Transport

The sweeping realization of the Nazis' decades-old ideological and political intention of finally "annihilating" the Jewish people draws closer and closer. Shortly after the beginning of the war they refer for the first time explicitly to the railroad as the means of transporting people to their death:

On September 21, 1939, following the first massacres of Polish Jews, the SS general and head of the Reich Security Service Reinhard Heydrich issues the following command to death squad leaders: " . . . the first preparatory measure toward the ultimate goal must be a concentration from the country to the larger cities. This is to be carried out as quickly as possible. . . . In this connection care must be taken that only cities that are railroad junctions or at least located on railroad lines are identified as points of concentration."

In January 1941 the SS battalion leader Paul Zapp adds a comment to a speech manuscript for his "boss," SS general Heinrich Himmler: "The complete resolution of the Jewish question can only be considered if we are successful in decisively striking world Jewry. The political and diplomatic leadership of Adolf Hitler has laid the groundwork for the European solution to the Jewish question. From this point on, what must be tackled is the solution of the world Jewish question." The indication here is that the deportation plans of the Nazi regime have as their goal a global "final solution," which the planned war of conquest is to introduce and make possible. Since the Nazis themselves are aiming for the world domination that they impute to their Jewish victims, the expulsion of the European Jews alone is not enough for the Nazi criminals. For them, this is only the preparatory stage to the "complete annihilation of world Jewry."

On March 12, 1941, Adolf Eichmann is already speaking routinely to his cohorts of the "without question impending final solution to the Jewish question" and thus justifies a ban on Jewish emigration from all occupied territories. Germany is to become the first European country "purified of Jews."

Himmler's personal physician Felix Kersten testified that Himmler had said in spring of 1941 that "the Jews must be exterminated to the last man by the end of the war. This is the explicit wish and command of the Führer." In May 1941 Heydrich has six mobile death squads set up and trained for their murderous tasks. With their order of June 6, 1941, high-ranking generals of the army back the planned war crimes. The General Plan East of June 24 provides for the systematic deportation, starvation, or killing of as many as 30 million people.

At the very beginning of the war against Russia on June 22, 1941[16], the state-sponsored persecution of the Jews escalates. The death squads begin their mass shootings of Jewish men in Soviet territory. In the overcrowded Polish ghettos tens of thousands are already dying of hunger and disease. The willingness of the Nazis to carry out the "final solution" earlier and more quickly increases. On August 1, 1941, Gestapo boss Heinrich Müller instructs the death squad leaders to regularly report their results to the Reich Chancellary. From August 15 on, Jewish women and children are indiscriminately murdered as well.

---

16. From this point on, during the war of extermination fought by the German army and the Nazi special troops, 5.7 million Soviet soldiers were taken prisoner. Since they were considered in the eyes of the Nazis as "sub-human" and "agents of the Jewish-Bolshevik international conspiracy," the German army had disempowered all existing conventions of war. At the eastern front, mass shootings by the army and the SS involving captured soldiers as well as partisans, were daily events. Every second Red Army soldier, as many as three million of them, died in German prison camps because of extremely bad treatment at the hands of the Nazis. In the case of captured soldiers from western European countries, the "death quota" amounted to 3.5 percent.

At the beginning of 1941, Hans-Adolf Prützmann, a high-ranking SS and police director in the Eastern Reich commissariat, responds to a subordinate's question as to where the Baltic Jews would be resettled by saying: "Not the way you think—they're going to be transported into the beyond." Around September 1941 the Nazis decide to murder all the European Jews they can get their hands on while the war was still continuing. At this point the term "final solution" signifies the execution of this goal in official language as well, although to the outside world it continues to be disguised as "resettlement" to distant territories in the east. Consequently, on September 5 and 6, 1941, 900 prisoners of war in the concentration camp Auschwitz I are gassed with the cyanide-based zyklon B as a test. In November, four of the six death squads are given gas trucks. Reports by the perpetrators themselves indicate that by March 1942 a total of almost 600,000 Jews had been murdered—already about ten percent of all those brutally killed by the Nazis by 1945.

"*Jews must be exterminated to the last man by the end of the war*"

Otto Adolf Eichmann (1906-62) was an SS lieutenant colonel and, as head of a sub-department of the Security Service, in charge of organizing the expulsion and deportation of the Jews. This meant that he was in part responsible for the murder of around six million individuals in the extensive areas of Europe occupied by the Nazis. In May 1960 he was abducted by Israeli agents in Argentina and taken to Israel. In a trial that lasted several months he was sentenced to death and executed in Ramla (near Tel Aviv) in May 1962.

1942 – The Final Decision to Murder all Jews

At the so-called Berlin-Wannsee Conference of January 20, 1942, Heydrich presents his "overall outline" to leading representatives of all Nazi authorities, so as to officially initiate these accomplices into the plans for the mass murders that are already underway. The Nazi authorities are instructed to coordinate the measures for the "final solution" appropriately. Eichmann confesses to this literally during the trial in Jerusalem: "The terms 'killing' and 'eliminating' and 'annihilation' were spoken." According to conference minutes, the plan is to deport and/or kill eleven million Jews from Europe and North Africa, including those from countries not conquered by Germany. On April 19, 1942, Himmler orders "the resettlement of the entire Jewish population of the General Government (German-occupied Poland) by December 31, 1942."

From now on the death trains from Germany and the conquered territories begin to roll to the now-ready annihilation camps. At the loading ramps there, those who had been packed into the freight cars[17] like animals are now "selected." In each instance some are immediately gassed, others later, and the corpses are burned.

---

17. The freight car on display in Fagen Museum, built in 1899, was one of those used to transport people to concentration camps. Previous to this, it had been used to ship all sorts of goods. It is probable that the almost 120-year-old boxcar also served to transport troops to and from the front during the First World War.

Aryan Pass

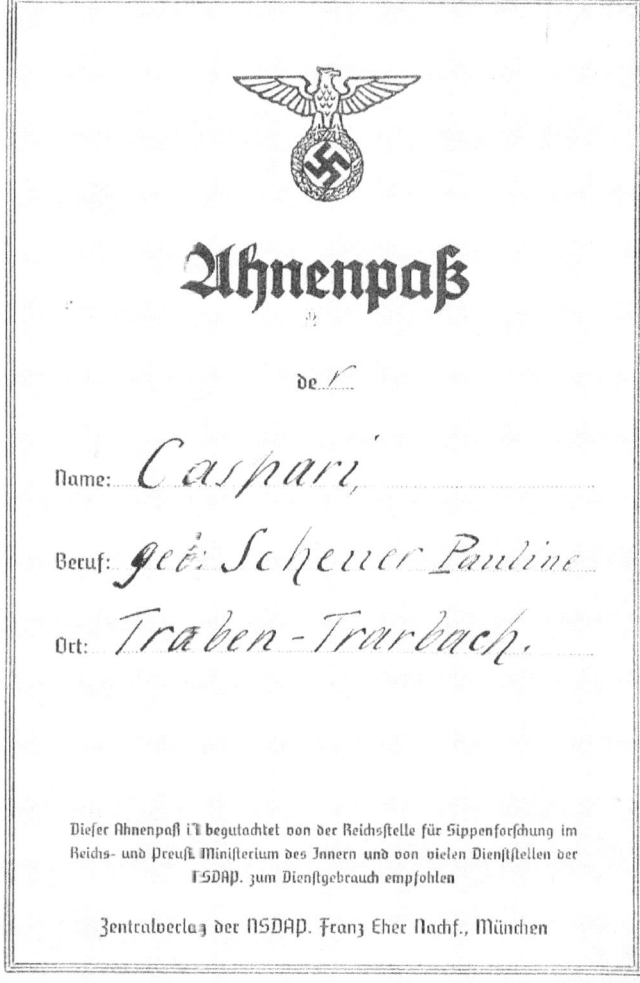

The "ancestor pass" pictured above was a document that Germans had to use in the Nazi regime to prove their "Aryan" origin. The disentitlement of Jewish citizens and others who were, according to Nazi "racial doctrine," not "of German blood" began in April 1933 with this "Aryan certificate." The basis in law for this pass was the so-called Aryan clause: only those who could prove descent from non-Jewish grandparents were considered Aryan.

The picture shows the "ancestor pass" of Fiede Caspari's paternal grandmother. Pauline Caspari (née Scheuer) was the wife of Friedrich Caspari, the publisher and editor of a small newspaper in the central Mosel region. Through the Nazis' "text-editor law" of October 1933, all journalists were degraded to the status of servants of the state. Journalists had to furnish an Aryan certificate for themselves and their spouses. From 1934 on, this group of persons was expanded to include all state and communal employees, as well as doctors, members of the legal profession, university students and schoolchildren in the upper grades. In September 1935, with the advent of the Nuremberg Laws, an Aryan certificate was required of all citizens of the German Reich. These regulations, which bordered on madness, deprived Jews step by step of every civil right.

1933 to 1945 – The Horror of the Concentration Camps

In the very first years of the Nazi dictatorship and up to the early summer of 1934, organizations sympathetic to the Nazis, especially the SA, construct several hundred detention camps everywhere in Germany in addition to the existing prisons. Shortly thereafter the notorious SS takes over the supervision of the camps, where political opponents of the Nazi regime are held illegally in "protective custody."

By the middle of 1933 around 26,000 people are already held in these camps. Among the first inmates are many politicians of the opposition, such as Social Democrats and Socialists, along with pastors and intellectuals who oppose Hitler. The persecution and annihilation madness of the Nazis later affects Sinti and Roma, homosexuals, and thousands of mentally and physically handicapped people, including several hundred children.

On September 21, 1939 it was decided by the Berlin Security Service main headquarters to deport all of the approximately 30,000 Sinti and Roma from the Reich into occupied Poland. A designated part of Poland known at the "General Government" was planned as a gigantic detention area for forced laborers working for the armaments industry. Ghettos and concentration camps were established in this area. Thousands of people, categorized as "racially inferior," were taken there starting in 1940 and had to live packed together in the tightest of quarters. From 1942 on, transports from there to the death camps ensued.

Beginning in 1932, homosexuals were sentenced on the basis of Paragraph 175 of the Penal Code, which was made more severe in 1935. By the beginning of 1945 approximately 60,000 men were sentenced to imprisonment and put into prisons, penal camps, and concentration camps. The systematic "hunt" by the Nazis for homosexuals had begun in Berlin with raids conducted by the Secret Police (Gestapo). Hundreds were caught unawares in gay bars, arrested, and taken to prisons and concentration camps without trial. There they had to wear a pink triangle, an insignia that marked them as homosexuals. There is considerable variation in the estimates of the number of gay men who died during the Nazi period, but research indicates that between 10,000 an 15,000 were taken to concentration camps and not released, and that a good half of these lost their lives.

A research project by the German Federal Archive in 2002 largely confirmed the previous estimates of the number of victims of the "euthanasia" conducted under the Nazi regime: approximately 200,000 emotionaly disturbed, mentally handicapped, or otherwise socially "different" people were murdered between 1939 and 1945. They died in gas chambers, from medical experimentation, or by starvation.

The concentration camps, increasingly established from 1934 on in other European countries, especially Poland, parallel to the Nazis' successful military campaigns in those countries, were lawless areas completely separated from the outer world. In total there were 24 gigantic main concentration camps, with ultimately over 1,000 smaller camps under their command. Added to this number were additional detention stations, which were not directly connected to the system of concentration camps, but which can also be classified as prison camps. Experts at the Holocaust Memorial Museum in Washington estimate that there were around 42,500 Nazi camps altogether, including prisoner-of-war camps, forced-labor camps, ghettos and so-called Jewish houses, houses of forced prostitution, and lodgings for euthanasia victims.

In eastern Europe alone the SS set up 600 areas known at the time as "ghettos," in which at least four million people were interned. These "living districts" were for the most part intended for use only in connection with the intended "final solution." Given the lack of sufficient railroad freight cars, these enclosed and fenced-in ghettos also served as temporary housing for those who would later be transported, in sub-human conditions, to the concentration camps.

Volker Ullrich writes in *Die Zeit* of April 14, 2016: "To each his own' – this is the inscription at the gate to the Buchenwald concentration camp, which was constructed in the summer of 1937 near Weimar. The meaning of the old Roman legal principle suum cuique was thereby cynically reversed. Repainted in red every year and easily legible by the prisoners during roll call, the inscription was intended as a daily reminder that they were excluded from the "community of the people" and were at the mercy of the capriciousness of the SS. – The first camp commander, Karl Koch, had given the prisoner and former Bauhaus student Franz Ehrlich the task of designing the lettering, not suspecting that the letters would be a throwback to those of his Dessau teachers. In this way, one element of the Bauhaus modernism outlawed as 'degenerate' by the National Socialists was smuggled into the camp – as an act of silent resistance."

Today, the permanent memorial exhibition established in 2016 at Buchenwald[18] documents the terrible fate of its Nazi victims. The exhibition also shows, however, the extent to which the camp was a part of everyday German life, and how individual citizens and companies profited from the camp "enterprise."

---

18. Possibility Fagen-Exhibiton shows a video interview with Christine Lieberknecht (born in Weimar in 1958) on the concentration camp Buchenwald. Ms. Lieberknecht, a CDU politician, was active as a Lutheran pastor until 1990 and, since the reunification, a representative in the state parliament of Thuringia. From October 2009 until December 2014, she was prime minister of the Free State of Thuringia and Chair of the State CDU.

Recommended in connection with the exhibition: The German-language novel "Wintermänner" by the Danish writer Jesper Bugge Kold (born in 1972). The novel unmasks the terrible consequences of the so-called Nazi ideology. Two brothers from Hamburg lead normal middle-class lives until they become fatefully sucked into the vortex of the Nazi movement. As an officer in the supply units of the Second World War (railroad!), Karl experiences the horrors at the front. Gerhard remains in Germany, but is partially responsible for transporting Jews (by railroad, in freight cars!) to concentration and death camps. He ultimately rises to the position of commanding officer of the concentration camp in Neuengamme, near Hamburg. After the war he flees to South America. - The novel is available in German as a paperback and in E-version through Amazon. An English-language translation, titled "Winter Men," was appeared in 2016.

1933 to 1945 – Resistance and the Rescue of Jews

Although millions of Germans applauded Hitler and his sinister fellow Nazis to the bitter end and believed in "final victory," there were in this fearful Nazi period thousands of "good" Germans. These were people who resisted the system, if only through their words (that alone was dangerous!) or by open resistance through their actions. And there were numerous Germans who helped their persecuted Jewish fellow citizens by hiding them from the Nazis and saving them from death in the concentration camps.

To name just a few of the "brave souls" who offered resistance and sacrificed their lives in doing so: the brother-and-sister student pair Hans and Sophie Scholl (with their action program "White Rose"), the officers of July 20, 1944, centered around Count Stauffenberg, who tried to remove Hitler with assassination attempts, and the Protestant pastor Dietrich Bonhoeffer, who can be cited as representative of other oppositional clergymen. Unfortunately, in the case of each of the above, their active resistance did not succeed; they were all murdered by the SS or the Gestapo, having previously been condemned by the most vicious judge of the Nazi dictatorship, Roland Freisler, the head of the "People's Court." Judgments spoken at that time "in the name of the people" are examples of juristic blasphemy, in that they turned murderous injustice into justice.

Hans & Sophie Scholl

Hans and Sophie Scholl are considered symbolic representatives of the humanistically-oriented resistance within Germany against the totalitarian Nazi regime. Hans (b. 1918) and Sophie (b. 1921) were the leading members of the student resistance group known as "White Rose." While distributing pamphlets on February 18, 1943 at the University of Munich, they were surprised by the caretaker Jakob Schmid and denounced to the Gestapo. Only four days later, on February 22, they were condemned to death and executed by guillotine on the same day. Moments before his execution, Hans Scholl shouted out: "Long live freedom!" The prison guards were amazed that both Hans and Sophie went to their deaths with such great composure.

Claus Ph. M. Schenk v. Stauffenberg

Count von Stauffenberg was an officer in the German army and one of the central personalities of the military resistance to National Socialism during the Second World War. Colonel von Stauffenberg, a main actor in the failed assassination attempt of July 20, 1944 against Hitler, was responsible for placing the bomb at the Wolfsschanze (Wolf's Lair), one of Hitler's headquarters in East Prussia. After the failure of the coup d'état, known as "Operation Walküre," he was summarily executed after midnight on July 21 in Berlin by General Friedrich Fromm. There are differences of opinion concerning Stauffenberg's life and career. He began as a "passionate German nationalist" and was completely in sympathy with National Socialism. Only when the war was almost lost did he recognize the criminal nature of the regime, and it was predominantly because of the hopelessness of the military situation that he became actively involved in the resistance movement.

Dietrich Bonhoeffer

Dietrich Bonhoeffer (1906-1945) was a Lutheran theologian and a distinguished representative of the Confessing Church. He is reckoned today to be one of the most revered of the resistance fighters against National Socialism. At the very beginning of the Nazi dictatorship, in April 1933, he publicly expressed his opposition to the persecution of the Jews and became involved in the church struggle against the "German Christians" and the new pro-Aryan laws. Beginning in 1935, he headed the pastors' seminary of the Confessing Church in Finkenwalde, which continued to exist illegally until 1940. In 1938 he became part of the resistance led by Admiral Canaris. In 1940 he was banned from speaking publicly, and in 1941 from writing. He was arrested on April 5, 1943 and two years later, after being falsely accused of involvement in the assassination attempt of July 20, 1944, became one of the last Nazi opponents to be executed.

Also among the critics of Hitler and the murderous procedures of the SS is Admiral Wilhelm Canaris, head of counter-intelligence, who was part of the Stauffenberg circle. Even before the assassination attempt of July 20 he was suspended from the service, in part because he employed Jews in his area of work. Many of these he sent abroad as agents and thereby saved their lives. In addition, he criticized the actions of the death squads in Poland. He, too, was executed following the assassination attempt of July 20, 1944.

In 1981, the writer Will Berthold (1924-2000) published a book called "The 42 Assassination Attempts against Hitler." Here he describes all the failed attempts on Hitler's life, whether planned or carried out. Other sources refer to 39 documented attempts. Hitler himself spoke of a "Providence" that saved him from such attacks.

On December 31, 1941, Abba Kovner, a Lithuanian-Israeli writer and partisan leader against National Socialism, appealed to the Jews in the entire world to offer resistance. He criticized the Nazi victims for allowing themselves "to be led like sheep to the slaughter." Thus arose the clichéd notion that all the victims failed to resist. It was not until the 1980s that research modified and corrected this view.

Only relatively few Jews during the Nazi regime had any idea of the extent of the fate that was planned for them. The information about mass annihilation camps that increasingly began to circulate in the ghettos of Poland, Lithuania, and White Russia was for the most part considered rumor. A plan to exterminate all the Jews seemed unbelievable to most people in the beginning, if only because of the scale of what was actually happening. Many believed that they would at least be able to survive as slave workers until the Germans were defeated.

In the post-war debate, the German historian of Polish origin Arno Lustiger[19] (1924-2012) gave numerous examples that contradict the American historian Raul Hilberg, who represented the position that Jewish resistance against the Nazi regime was inconsequential. Lustiger produced significant contributions in the area of research and reappraisal of the history of Jewish resistance.

In January 1945, as Soviet troops approached, Arno Lustiger was part of the forced march to the concentration camp Groß-Rosen in Lower Silesia, during which only half of the 4,000 prisoners survived. From there he was taken to Buchenwald and then to another concentration camp, in Langenstein-Zwieberge near Halberstadt. According to Lustiger, the life expectancy of the prisoners there was three to four weeks. In April this concentration camp was also abandoned as American troops were about to arrive, and another forced march began. Lustiger managed to escape, but fell into the hands of members of the Volkssturm, formed in 1944 of mostly older men and young boys. Yet he was able to escape again and, found by American soldiers, served in the U.S. Army as an interpreter. Following his discharge from the army he remained in Germany and built up a successful business in ladies' wear. Only after "40 years of silence," as he himself formulated it, did he begin to publish works on Jewish history of the 20th century. He is a co-founder of the Jewish congregation of Frankfurt am Main.

The uprising in the Warsaw ghetto (April 19 to May 16, 1943) provided an impetus for Jewish resistance in general. It was organized by the Jewish fighting organization "ZOB" as the Nazis

---

19. Arno Lustiger shared the fate of many Jews, but was able to survive in several concentration camps. His father, David Lustiger, was a councilman and proprietor of a concern in Bedzin that made machines for the production of bread. When the war began, the business was "Aryanized," though the owner stayed on at first as an employee. At the beginning of 1943, when the Jewish population was interned in the ghetto of Bedzin, the Lustiger family was able to hide in a cellar. In August the ghetto was cleared and the inhabitants were deported to Auschwitz-Birkenau. The family managed to end up in the forced labor camp Annaberg in Silesia, but there the family members were separated. At age 19, Arno was first taken to the camp at Ottmuth, then to one in Blechhammer, both exterior camps of Auschwitz. Arnold's father David was murdered in Auschwitz-Birkenau.

were about to completely dissolve the ghetto and send any remaining Jews to death camps, most often Treblinka. The underground organization had received weapons through couriers between the "Aryan" part of Warsaw and the barricaded ghetto and its fighters were able to inflict high casualties on the SS soldiers until they returned with tanks and artillery. In spite of the superior strength of the Nazi forces, the resistance groups managed to hold on for four weeks in house-to-house fighting. Those who finally surrendered were shot; only a few were able to escape through the sewers.

Resistance groups formed in other ghettos as well, some of which started uprisings and helped their inhabitants to escape. There were also revolts in several of the camps, such as Treblinka (May 1943) and Sobibor (October 1943). In Auschwitz-Birkenau there were 700 attempted escapes, 300 of them successful. In October 1944, the Jewish "special command" (responsible for taking care of the bodies burned in the ovens) revolted and blew up part of Crematorium IV, using explosives smuggled in by women. The 250 prisoners who tried to escape were captured and killed.

Throughout Europe, thousands of Jews who had hidden away successfully took part in partisan battles against the German occupiers, especially in France, Belgium, the Netherlands, Italy, the Balkan states, and Greece. In eastern Europe, especially Poland with its predominantly Catholic population, Jews who had escaped from concentration camps or ghettos were seldom able to join existing partisan groups, since many of those who opposed the Nazis were also hostile to Jews. For this reason Jewish partisan units sometimes formed there and proved to be determined and motivated fighters despite their initial inexperience.

The advancing Red Army sometimes gave them preference in supplying them with weapons, especially for the "war on rails," with attacks and sabotage activities against the railroad transport of the German army to the eastern front. In North Africa, Jewish resistance fighters in "Operation Torch" stormed the presumedly impregnable fortress at Algier, thus offering decisive assistance to the landing of the Allies and its successful campaign against the German North Africa Corps.

German Jews as Allied Soldiers

Many Jews, able to emigrate to the safety of other countries in the 1930s and at the beginning of the war, joined the Allied troops. In a few of the armies there were separate Jewish units, for example the Jewish Brigade of the British Army with its 10,000 German-speaking Jews; there were also about 9,500 in the United States military. Towards the end of the war, the Jewish relief agency Beriha (Hebrew for "escape") was founded and helped around 250,000 Jews from eastern European countries to flee between 1944 and 1948. After the war, these German Jews often served as translators for the Allies in occupied Germany. It is estimated that as many as 1.5 million Jews from all over Europe were involved in the regular military and partisan war against the Nazi regime.

Even in Germany itself several thousand Jews survived. These include not only displaced persons and so-called "quarter Jews," but also those who were hidden, at great risk to themselves, by German citizens opposed to the system. According to recent reliable sources several thousand were able to "disappear" with the help and support of others. Well-known Holocaust survivors include the actor and writer Michael Degen[20] and the TV star, moderator, and entertainer Hans Rosenthal[21]. A television film from 2006 called "They weren't all murderers," based on the 1999 biography of Michael Degen, portrays the fate of people who were given help during the years of horror.

---

20. Michael Degen was born in Chemnitz in 1932 as the son of Jakob Degen, a professor of languages and a merchant of Russian-Jewish origin, and his wife Anna. In 1933 they moved with him and his older brother Adolf from Chemnitz to Berlin-Tiergarten. In the winter of 1939-40, his brother was sent via Denmark and Sweden to Palestine in order to save him from the National Socialist reign of terror. His father was deported by the Gestapo in 1939. Though he was able to survive the concentration camp Sachsenhausen in spite of severe injuries, he died shortly after his release from the results of the torture he had been subjected to in 1940. Michael Degen continued to attend the Jewish school until it was closed in 1942. In the face of the forced removals of their neighbors by the Gestapo in 1943, his mother decided on the spur of the moment to save herself and her son from the clutches of the Nazis. During their escape they had to change their hiding place eight times, using false identities, until they finally were able to stay with non-Jewish friends at a garden plot in the Berlin suburb of Kaulsdorf and survive.

21. Hans Rosenthal (1925-1987) grew up in a Jewish family in the Prenzlauer Berg section of Berlin and experienced as a child the growing persecution by the Nazis. His father, Kurt Rosenthal, died of kidney failure in 1937 at the age of 36, shortly after he had been fired by the Deutsche Bank as a "non-Aryan." Following the death of his mother from cancer in 1941, Hans ended up in an orphanage with his brother Gert and was given the compulsory name Hans Israel Rosenthal. His brother was deported to Riga in 1942 at the age of ten and was murdered a few days later in the concentration camp at Majdanek. Other family members were likewise murdered during the Holocaust. In 1940, Hans was put into forced labor by the Nazis. Among other things, he worked as a gravedigger and did factory piecework in Berlin. In March 1943 he was able to hide in the small garden installation "Trinity" and survived until the end of the war. He was cared for in his hiding place by three non-Jewish Berlin women: Ida Jauch, an acquaintance of his mother's, Maria Schönebeck, and Emma Harndt. Ida Jauch was honored posthumously in October 2015 in Israel as a "righteous one among the peoples."

"The Path of the Righteous Among the Nations"

In even greater numbers, as many as several thousand, individuals of courage and daring saved Jewish people and concentration camp inmates from certain death. Three such examples are Sir Nicholas George Winton, Oskar Schindler, and Folke Bernadotte, Count of Wisborg (Please see p. 64: Further Consequences of the War in the German-Danish Region).

Nicholas George Winton (1909-2015), a British citizen of German-Jewish heritage (original name: Wertheimer), organized the rescue of 669 Jewish children of mostly German-Czech background from the threatening Holocaust shortly before the beginning of the Second World War. Winton was involved in international banking and had paid a visit to Prag at Christmas in 1938. At the time, the capital city was overrun with refugees as a result of the German occupation of the Sudetenland. Sensitized because of his own background, he organized entry permits for children after his return to London; following the November pogroms in Germany, this had been made possible through a British law for children under the age of 17 (the Refugee Children's Movement). Winton was philanthropically active even at an advanced age and was honored for this with the Order of the British Empire. For decades he said nothing about his good deeds; then his wife found relevant material in the attic of their house in 1988 and let the public know what had happened. Winton was 106 years old when he died on July 1, 2015.

Oskar Schindler (1908-1974), a German-Moravian entrepreneur, with the help of his wife saved 1,200 Jewish forced laborers who were employed by him from being murdered in the death camps. After the German attack on Poland, Schindler, a Nazi party member, took over a sheet metal factory in Krakow, hoping to profit from the war. By the end of 1942, the business had become a munitions factory, and hence essential to the war effort. The factory employed 800 workers, including 370 Jews from the Krakow ghetto. Out of sympathy for the plight of the helpless Jews, Schindler tried to save as many as possible from death in the concentration camps. He described his forced laborers as essential, since their deportation would slow down work in the factory. He was not above lying, falsifying documents, or paying bribes, and frequently secured food for his workers at his own expense on the black market. When the Krakow ghetto was demolished in March 1943, Schindler's production was moved to the forced labor camp at Plaszow, where his Jewish workers lived in their own separate camp with relatively little harassment by the SS. In yet another move, in October 1944, the factory ended up in Brünnlitz in Moravia; for this move, he was allowed additional Jewish workers—those on the "list" mentioned in the film "Schindler's List." None of Schindler's workers were ever deported to death camps.

Folke Bernadotte, Count of Wisborg (1895-1948), was a Swedish diplomat and nobleman. During World War II he negotiated the release of about 31,000 prisoners from German concentration camps including 450 Danish Jews from the Theresienstadt camp. After the war, Bernadotte was unanimously chosen to be the United Nations Security Council mediator in the Arab–Israeli conflict of 1947–1948. He was assassinated in Jerusalem in 1948 by the militant Zionist group Lehi while pursuing his official duties. - While vice-president of the Swedish Red Cross in 1945, Bernadotte attempted to negotiate an armistice between Germany and the Allies. He also led several rescue missions in Germany for the Red Cross. During the autumns of 1943 and 1944, he organized prisoner exchanges which brought home 11,000 prisoners from Germany via Sweden.

In the spring of 1945, Bernadotte was in Germany when he met Heinrich Himmler, who was briefly appointed commander of an entire German army following the assassination attempt on Hitler the year before. Bernadotte had originally been assigned to retrieve Norwegian and Danish POWs in Germany. He returned on 1 May 1945, the day after Hitler's death. Following an interview, the Swedish newspaper *Svenska Dagbladet* wrote that Bernadotte succeeded in rescuing 15,000 people from German concentration camps, including about 8000 Danes and Norwegians and 7000 women of French, Polish, Czech, British, American, Argentinian, and Chinese nationalities. The missions took around two months, and exposed the Swedish Red Cross staff to significant danger, both due to political difficulties and by taking them through areas under Allied bombing.

The mission became known for its buses, painted entirely white except for the Red Cross emblem on the side, so that they would not be mistaken for military targets. In total it included 308 personnel (about 20 medics and the rest volunteer soldiers), 36 hospital buses, 19 trucks, seven passenger cars, seven motorcycles, a tow truck, a field kitchen, and full supplies for the entire trip, including food and gasoline, none of which was permitted to be obtained in Germany. A count of 21,000 people rescued included 8,000 Danes and Norwegians, 5,911 Poles, 2,629 French, 1,615 Jews, and 1,124 Germans. (Please, see p. 63, photo of "White Buses".)

After Germany's surrender, the White Buses mission continued in May and June and about 10,000 additional liberated prisoners were thus evacuated. Bernadotte recounted the White Buses mission in his book The End. My Humanitarian Negotiations in Germany in 1945 and Their Political Consequences, published on June 15, 1945 in Swedish. In the book, Bernadotte recounts his negotiations with Himmler and others, and his experience at the Ravensbrück concentration camp.

"The Path of the Righteous among the Nations," inaugurated in 1963 in the Holocaust Memorial Yad Vashem, is lined with trees that are planted for the "righteous." The term refers to gentiles and organizations that opposed the Nazi regime in order to save the lives of Jews. Their names and countries of origin are inscribed on plaques next to the trees. Examples are the above-described Oskar Schindler, Chiune Sugihara (a Japanese diplomat in Lithuania), the German industrialist Berthold Beitz, and Giorgio Perlasca, an Italian businessman in Budapest. Thousands of Jews were saved as the result of these men's efforts. The costs of the memorial site are borne by Germany.

1936 to 1939 – The Bombing War begins in Spain

Return to the War: The rapid development of military and flying techniques has resulted in the "modern" bombing war—not only against military targets, but against civilian populations as well. The bombardment of cities still played a subordinate role in the First World War. From August 1914 to November 1918 French and British airplanes undertook air attacks on German cities, though these led to relatively minor loss of lives and material damage. In that war, the Allies also wanted to destroy the starting and landing fields of German airships that were dropping bombs on England. Shortly before the armistice of November 1918, an air offensive against the Rhein-Ruhr area and Berlin was planned for the beginning of 1919. In this particular scheme, the expected effects on the morale of the civilian population due to attacks by heavy bombers was a major consideration, one that became more and more important during the Second World War.

Two decades later the Nazi war machine struck with full force in the Spanish Civil War, through aerial bombardments that frequently injured non-combatants. Thousands were killed by German air force bombers, and the Basque capital of Guernica was reduced to rubble by the infamous Condor Legion in April 1937. These early events from 1936 to 1939 showed the full aggressivity of Hitler's military machine. The Spanish Civil War, with its decisive support of Franco's Fascists by German troops, was a warning to the peace-loving world that went unheeded for the most part. Only a few months after the end of German involvement in Spain, Hitler's attack on Poland in September 1939 unleashed the Second World War.

1939 to 1945 – Expansion of the Bombing War

The first civilian bombing victims of Nazi Germany in the war were the citizens of Warsaw and Coventry. The fire bombings of Warsaw in September 1939 destroyed large areas of the city and resulted in an estimated 20,000 to 25,000 civilian deaths. Perhaps even more infamous was the first bombing of Coventry on November 14, 1940. Ostensibly an attack on an aircraft engine factory and other military production sites, the raid by the dreaded Stuka dive-bombers and Heinkel heavy bombers destroyed over 4,000 residences in the inner city, at least one irreplaceable cultural landmark, the medieval St. Michael's Cathedral, and killed 568 residents. A second air attack on the city not quite five months later, on April 8, 1941, claimed over 600 lives.

In 1944 and 1945, London and Antwerp in Belgium were hit several times by V-2 rockets launched from north Germany. Since the end of the 1930s, German engineers under the direction of Wernher von Braun—who was to play a leading role in the U.S. space program after the war—developed a variety of rockets. Ultimately it was the A-4, renamed V-2 for "Vergeltungswaffe" ("retaliation weapon"), that had the most success. Fortunately, the A-9 and A-10 rockets, with a projected range long enough to reach the United States, were never built. By contrast, the V-2, with its 2,000-pound explosive payload, had a range of 400 kilometers and could reach London in 320 seconds.

The First V-2 Against London on September 7, 1944

The first V-2 was launched against the British capital on September 7, 1944; by the end of March 1945, over 3,000 were fired, with targets in England, Belgium, and France. They were silent and struck without warning. In total the attacks killed between 8,000 and 12,000 people, mainly in London and Antwerp. The deaths of an additional 12,000 concentration camp prisoners must be added to the total of victims; in 1943 and 1944, these slave laborers worked under the most inhumane conditions imaginable to build an underground rocket factory in mine tunnels in the Harz Mountains. If there had been additional development time, it is conceivable that the V-rockets could have become the "wonder weapons" that the Nazi military and many civilians hoped would turn the tide of the war. The counter-measures of the Allies' Operation Crossbow, which was directed at all areas of V-weapon production, transportation, and deployment, helped to prevent this from happening. The psychological effects of Nazi propaganda were enormous: in Germany, the belief among many soldiers and civilians of a "final victory" was strengthened, while in England and Belgium the necessity of victory over the Nazi regime was confirmed.

Those Who Sow the Wind, Will Reap the Whirlwind

Those who sow the wind, will reap the whirlwind: from 1940 on and especially in the last months of the war, Germany is bombed on an almost daily basis by Allied air power. Bombs rain from the bomb bays of thousands of planes, predominantly on the Reich's largest cities, causing countless deaths and terrible destruction. The British Royal Air Force and, from January 1943 on, the United States Air Force, fly approximately 1.4 million sorties against Nazi Germany. Nearly two million tons of bombs are dropped, and hundreds of thousands of civilians are killed; almost one out of five German families is homeless.

One month after the bombardment of the English city of Coventry at the end of 1940, the RAF responds with its first carpet bombing. A squadron of 134 planes appears over Mannheim. With "only" 34 dead and over 1,200 bombed-out residents, the effect is relatively limited. But as the war drags on, escalated more and more by Hitler's commands, the Allies intensify their bombing runs. For the most part, American bombers attack by day, and the RAF by night. The Soviet air force is active in the area of the eastern front.

With the new strategy of intensified bombing in place, Major General Arthur Harris, the chief of the British bomber command, selects a target in Schleswig-Holstein: the militarily insignificant Hanseatic city of Lübeck on the Baltic Sea. On March 28, as the RAF drops 300 tons of bombs on the city, the historic city center goes up in flames. At the end of May, almost 1,000 bombers destroy large parts of Cologne; the world-famous cathedral is damaged, but remains standing. In 1943 the large-scale attacks on Berlin begin. At the end of July 1943, Operation Gomorrah turns the proud Hanseatic city of Hamburg, so beloved by many Britons, into a raging inferno.[22] More than 30,000 people die.

Not until 1944 do the centers of the armaments industry become the major goals of Allied bombing. In 1945, as the Allied armies are already fighting on German soil, the war from the air reaches its greatest intensity, thereby putting great pressure on German troops, who will not

---

22. Among others, the mother of Gitta Reppmann experienced and survived the fire-bombing of Hamburg. At the time, Gertrud Ortmann happened to be visiting her future mother-in-law in the part of the city called Rahlstedt.

give up the struggle. The German will to hold out is spurred on by Hitler's calls to duty and by standard Nazi slogans ("fight to the last man!").

An equally horrific catastrophe at the end of the war: the torpedoing of the refugee ship "Wilhelm Gustloff" by a Soviet submarine in the Baltic Sea on January 30, 1945. The ship was overloaded with around 10,000 German refugees from the eastern territories. Only 1,200 survived the sinking.

Severe Air Attacks - 1945

Cologne Downtown, 1945: The world famous Cologne Cathedral, next to the main train station the only building that was not totally destroyed.

January 29: In non-stop attacks, around 2,000 Allied bombers strike railroad facilities in German cities, including Hamm, Münster, Krefeld, Koblenz, and Siegen. (Personal memory: Fiede Caspari's grandmother in Koblenz is buried in rubble, but is rescued; Elisabeth Maxeiner had turned over a bathtub in her apartment and crawled under it.)

February 3: The U.S. Air Force drops more than 2,500 tons of bombs on the city center of Berlin, damaging numerous government buildings. Among the 2,600 dead is Roland Freisler, the president of the infamous "People's Court."

February 13: The Baroque city of Dresden with its world-famous edifices is laid waste by at least 1,000 RAF and U.S. bombers. On this raid 35,000 people are killed.

Severe Air Attacks - 1945

February 26: The heaviest day-time attack to date: 1,100 U.S. planes drop almost 2,900 tons of bombs on Berlin.

February 27: Within 20 minutes, 435 British bombers drop 1,500 tons of explosive- and fire-bombs on Mainz. The death toll is 1,200, 86 percent of the inner city is destroyed.

March 2: Cologne is softened up for ground attack by another bombardment; after a total of 262 air attacks from 1941 on, the city is taken by American forces.

March 12: A U.S. attack on the German naval base at Swinemünde claims 23,000 lives.

March 14: During an air attack on rail facilities near Bielefeld, the British put into action for the first time their 10-ton precision bomb "Grand Slam," creating subterranean shock waves.

March 16: RAF attack on the militarily insignificant city of Würzburg.

March 18: U.S. planes drop 4,000 tons of bombs on Berlin.

April 3: Air attack on the Baltic naval harbor of Kiel; the heavy cruiser "Admiral Hipper" is sunk.

April 10: U.S. attack on Leipzig, which is taken by the U.S. Army shortly thereafter.

April 14: Potsdam is bombarded by 512 RAF planes: 5,000 dead and extremely heavy damage to historic buildings.

April 18: The RAF drops 5,000 tons of bombs on the North Sea island of Helgoland.

April 19: The final British air attack on Berlin.

April 25: The Soviet air force attacks the German capital, now surrounded by the Red Army, with almost 1,500 planes.

May 3: British bombing attack at the Bay of Lübeck near Neustadt: more than 7,000 concentration camp prisoners on ships are killed, including those on the luxury steamer "Cap Arcona."

(Please, compare Appendices 3 & 4, p. 84 and 86.)

1944 – D-Day, the Beginning of the End of the War

With the landing of the U.S. Fifth Corps on the coast of Normandy on June 6, 1944, the end of the Second World War in Europe and the liberation from the Nazis begins. The section of coast near Colleville-sur-Mer and Saint-Laurent-sur-Mer has gone down in history as the staging area of the legendary Operation Neptune. American and other Allied troops land on a beachhead ten kilometers in length named after the city of Omaha. The stretch of coastline to the west of it is given the name Utah Beach, and the three to the east are called Gold, Juno, and Sword Beach. Around 7,000 ships and boats cross the English Channel between England and France, transporting a 200,000-man army of Britons, Americans, Canadians, Frenchmen, and Poles. This fighting force is supported by parachutists who had already landed the night before. The resistance of the German army units is extremely intense. The troops who land at Omaha Beach suffer the greatest losses.

May 1945 – The End of the War: Surrender and Liberation

The "thousand-year" Nazi empire founders in a sea of blood and tears. When the weapons finally grow silent on May 8, a total of more than 60 million have died—killed in action at the European and North African fronts, murdered in the death camps, burned to death in nights of bombing, dead from hunger, cold, and violence while attempting to flee. An additional 17 million are considered missing without trace. As the world finds out what happened in the German name, not only in the camps, but in total, the anger of the people understandably first turns to the entire German people.

Only relatively few people survive the inconceivable horrors of the death camps, which are liberated from July 1944 (Majdanek) until May 1945 (Theresienstadt) by Soviet and western Allied troops. The camp at Auschwitz (liberated by the Soviets in January 1945) is neither the first nor the last to be liberated, and the whole process takes slightly over one year. Before the Allies reach the camps, tens of thousands of prisoners, considered a threat to the Nazi leadership and their personnel, are quickly murdered. Additional thousands are sent on death marches to other camps or to die at the side of the road. For this reason there are often only a few hundred survivors remaining when the camps are liberated.

The history of the death marches is told by survivors in select biographies in the multi-lingual Internet site of the International Auschwitz Committee. The site also contains an overview of the liberation of the camps.

1933 to 1946 – Emigration, Exile, Flight, and Expulsion

The historical events affecting the many thousands of people who had to leave or flee their homeland because of the Hitler regime are entwined with individual fates too numerous to be described in detail. As early as the 1930s, countless prominent German-speaking persons emigrate, for the most part to England, the United States, Switzerland, South America, Canada, and the Far East. It is not only Jewish Germans and Austrians who seek to escape the control of the Nazis, the racial persecution, the psychic suppression, and the physical violence. Among the émigrés are intellectuals, such as composers, musicians, writers, actors, and other artists and scientists of all types. After the Nazi takeover of the government, for example, more than 1,500 individuals active in the film industry leave German, Austria, and Bohemia-Moravia.

The flights and expulsions from the German eastern territories and from east central, eastern, and southeastern Europe during and after the end of the war affect the 12 to 14 million Germans resident there. They are the result of the war crimes committed in these parts of Europe during the Nazi period and the loss of territory as established by the victorious powers (United States, Soviet Union, Great Britain). Among those expelled in 1945-46 are several thousand Germans from Bohemia and Moravia who had lived in the former Czechoslovakia. These people move to the West, especially Bavaria, and hundreds emigrate to the United States, as their predecessors had done in the 19th century. Many settle in and around New Ulm, Minnesota, where today's *German-Bohemian Heritage Society* commemorates their origin.[23]

Flensburg: The Last Stop for Nazi Germany

In the spring of 1945, the SS begins to dismantle concentration camps in North Germany that are now in the Allies' lines of advance, with the intention of eradicating the proofs of their unprecedented crimes. The prison camps are burned down, weak and starving inmates are murdered, and the remaining prisoners are sent on long marches as potential hostages to as yet unoccupied regions. Some of these paths of suffering, for example from the camps in Stutthof (near Danzig) and Neuengamme (near Hamburg) come to their sad conclusion at the end of April and the beginning of May in Flensburg. This city is also the place to which high members of the Nazi regime retreat following Hitler's suicide.

Provisory Government Under Admiral Dönitz

While the capital city of the Reich collapses in street fighting and tens of thousands of Germans pay with their lives in the fight to the bitter end commanded by the Nazi regime, Hitler evades his responsibility on April 30 by committing suicide. Admiral Karl Dönitz, whom Hitler had appointed to be his successor, establishes a provisory government in Flensburg on the German-Danish border.

Dönitz empowers General Alfred Jodl (in charge of the conduct of the war from Norway to North Africa) to lead the surrender negotiations with General Dwight D. Eisenhower, commander in chief of the Allied forces in Europe, at the American headquarters in Reims. Jodl tries to delay the German surrender to the Red Army in order to make it possible for the Germans in the eastern territories to escape to the west, but is not successful.

---

23. Secretary Wade Olsen offers this background: "German-Bohemians are people who have either lived in or have ancestry in the outer rim of the Czech Republic. Once this region was part of the Holy Roman Empire of the German nation, when people moved and settled freely in Central Europe. When the nation of Czechoslovakia was created in 1919 out of the former Austrian crown colonies of Bohemia, Moravia and Slovakia, the German-speaking outer rim came to be known as the Sudetenland, named for the terrain that separates Germany from Bohemia. After World War II, three and one half million of these Germans from Sudetenland were forcibly expelled from their homeland and "resettled" throughout Germany. These, too, are German-Bohemians, although they prefer to be known as Sudeten-Germans. – Beginning in the early 1850s, and increasingly throughout the balance of the 19th century, there was a large chain migration to Minnesota and Wisconsin. Motivated by a string of immigrant letters, hundreds of immigrants joined their families and brought with them elements of the culture, crafts, traditions, music and values that characterize the descendents of these German-Bohemian immigrants to this day."
Internet information: www.germanbohemianheritagesociety.com/who-are-the-german-bohemians

On May 7, 1945, Jodl finally signs the unconditional surrender agreement for the German Reich, which goes into effect on the following day. The Soviet dictator Josef Stalin pushes for a repeat of the ceremony in his sphere of influence; on May 9, Field Marshal Wilhelm Keitel, chief of the supreme command of the German army, signs another surrender document at the Soviet headquarters in Berlin-Karlshorst. After more than five years of war in Europa, the guns are finally silent.

Although the surrender had already taken place on May 8, the Reich's naval war flag continues to fly until May 23 in Flensburg, when British troops put an end to the specter of Dönitz.

From left to right: Albert Speer, Minister of Armaments and War Production, and Hitler's chief architect; Grand Admiral Karl Dönitz; and Alfred Jodl, Chief of the Operations Staff of the Armed Forces High Command (Oberkommando der Wehrmacht), in front of the world media, May 23, 1945 in the backyard of the Flensburg main police station. The world media had been invited to take a photo of the last day of the Third Reich.

The Revenge of the Victors

After the end of the fighting the revenge of the victors begins, in retaliation for the enormous suffering brought on by the Germans and those who helped them. Around 14 million Germans are driven out; these are mostly women and girls, who are forced to pay for Hitler's war by suffering countless atrocities themselves, including rapes, plundering, and murder.

In the wake of forced labor, hunger, and sickness, nearly two million of the 3.2 million German prisoners of war return to Germany from the Soviet Union, the last 10,000 not until 1956. Once again freight cars are the means of transportation for the former soldiers as they return from the distant expanses of the East. The fate of more than a million German soldiers is still unknown today.

The end of the war, however, is not the cause of the flight of the refugees, their expulsion and loss of freedom; the reason for these consequences lies solely in the tyrannical rule that led to the war. May 8, 1945 may not be separated from January 30, 1933, the day of the transfer of power to Hitler, nor from the events that preceded and followed this date.[24]

Nazi Officers Flee to North Germany

At the end of the war, hundreds of former Nazi officers, SS members, war criminals, and hoodlums of the defeated system make their way in secret to safe regions of the world, or attempt at first to hide inside Germany. In the latter connection, Schleswig-Holstein becomes one of the largest areas of retreat for Nazi criminals. Around 30 "high-value" Nazi leaders and generals of the SS and the army, as well as a few hundred lower-ranking SS soldiers find temporary hiding places in the northernmost North of Germany. Many disguise themselves as civilians or as "ordinary" soldiers, such as SS Reichsführer Heinrich Himmler and the commandant of the Auschwitz concentration camp, SS Lieutenant Colonel Rudolf Höss, whose "colleague" Hans Bothmann, an SS captain and commandant of the death camp Chelmno/Kulmhof (Poland) would become the director of the Gestapo commissariat in Flensburg. SS Lieutenant General Richard Glücks, chief of inspection for all the concentration camps, also "saves" himself at the command of Himmler by going to Flensburg.

The above-mentioned Rudolf Höss found a network of helpers in Flensburg. Disguised as a simple marine with the name of Franz Lang, he lived in various locations, including one night in a building in Moltkestraße 21.[25]

Following the surrender, Höss, alias Franz Lang, found a job through the Flensburg employment office on a farm in the nearby village of Gottrupel. The father himself was still a prisoner of war at this time, and Höß becomes more or less a member of the family. Without knowing that he had been one of the Nazi regime's most terrible murderers, the farmer's family and the villagers described him as hard-working, modest, polite, and friendly.

After being discovered by the British officer Hanns Alexander, a Jewish emigrant of German extraction, Höß was arrested by the Military Police on March 11, 1946. During his detention he described a meeting with Himmler in July 1941 at which he was given, quite literally, "the clear order for the mass annihilation of the Jews." Handed over to Polish authorities, he was condemned for his deeds and, one year later, in March 1947, hanged on the gallows at Auschwitz, his former "domain."

---

24. Ulrich Herbert, Professor of Recent History in Freiburg, comments (in *Die Zeit*, No. 50/2015) on the fact that a new Hitler biography appears every few years: "It is a mistake to believe that one can understand the Nazi regime solely by examining Hitler, given the image of that regime which has been worked out in the meantime—an image that is multifaceted in its consideration of the number of persons and arenas involved."

25. In no. 6 Moltkestraße, only a few yards away, Yogi and Gitta Reppmann have had an apartment for over 20 years.

Höss & Hensel

Rudolf Höss: *The longest-serving commandant of Auschwitz concentration camp in World War II. He tested methods to accelerate Hitler's plan to systematically exterminate the Jewish population of Nazi-occupied Europe, known as the Final Solution. He created the largest installation for the continuous annihilation of human beings ever known. He was hanged in Auschwitz in 1947 following a trial in Warsaw.*

Flensburg had become the last capital of Nazi Germany after Hitler had committed suicide, April 30th, 1945. In the Flensburg police station Himmler, Commander of the SS, advised Höss to disguise himself among German Navy personnel. He evaded arrest for nearly a year. When captured by British troops on 11 March 1946 in Gottrupel, a village a mile away from Flensburg, he was disguised as a gardener and called himself Franz Lang. His wife, sister of Fritz Hensel, who feared that her son, Klaus, would be shipped off to the Soviet Union to be imprisoned or tortured, had told the British where he was.

Höss & Hensel

Drawing: Gerhard Fritz Hensel, 1910-1986, brother-in-law of Rudolf Höss, had visited his sister in Auschwitz for longer stays. He made drawings in Auschwitz, and supported Höss in Flensburg. After WWII, Hensel was an art teacher in the Flensburg high school 'Goethe-Schule' until 1972. His drawing 'Sola in Auschwitz' is in the archive of the concentration camp, Auschwitz. Many other Hensel drawings are in the collection of the German Historical Museum, Berlin.

The White-Washing of Nazi Crimes

Especially in the "retreat center" of Flensburg, but also in Schleswig-Holstein in general, many former Nazis who either had blood on their hands or were at least involved in making decisions with terrible consequences, were housed anonymously or sometimes quite openly and given lucrative service positions. This happened because of a certain "white-washing syndicate" that was involved in shady dealings.[26] The former Nazi hoodlums were sentenced to minor penalties by their old Nazi comrades, they talked their way out of things, were hidden and protected, false testimonies were given, they were exonerated from worse crimes - and, accepted by German post-war society, they subsequently led ordinary middle-class lives or occupied positions of power. It was not until much later that this situation was discussed and written about.

This particular burden from the post-war period also rests on the Germans. Hundreds of perpetrators and accomplices of the Nazi regime were indeed found guilty, but following the liberation many ended up in exalted positions again with the newly established (West)German authorities and institutions in spite of having been screened for involvement in culpable activities during the Nazi period. They found positions of responsibility in the young German democracy—in the justice system, in administrative positions, with the police, and in the medical professions. There are countless examples of this; one is Hermann Weinkauff (1894-1981), the first president of the Federal Supreme Court. He was appointed to this lofty and responsible office despite having taken part in a trial for violation of the Nazis'"blood protection law" in 1936 as a member of the Reich Supreme Court (Source: *Die Zeit*, No. 38/2015, p. 18).

It has only been since 2005 that 16 official commissions, established by German ministries and authorities and involving over 100 historians, have been carefully examining the Nazi past. An interim report from the beginning of 2016 is commented on by Martin Sabrow, the director of the Center for the Research of Contemporary History in an interview in *Die Zeit* (No. 7/11.02.2016, p. 17).

---

26. Source reference: Prof. Gerhard Paul, in his book "Mai 45 – Kriegsende in Flensburg" (2015).

Former Nazis in West German Public Offices

Sabrow points out that the number of former Nazis in the Federal Ministry of the Interior, the Foreign Office, and the Federal Ministry of Justice was especially great in the first years of the new Federal Republic (West Germany). The "degree of incrimination" amounted to 60 percent and more at that time. "Former Nazi party members were able to advance without problem in the Federal Ministry of Justice, but not in the Federal Office for the Defense of the Constitution," according to Sabrow. This was because the Allied Control Commission prevented a continuity of personnel to a certain extent. "The Americans did, of course, apply different standards," Sabrow said.

While great care was taken with the (then new) Constitutional department "that the office not become a Nazi enclave, they accepted at the same time that Reinhard Gehlen,[27] in his organization led by the CIA, and later as chief of the German Federal Intelligence Service, did not care a whit about the Nazi past of his co-workers." There were Nazi-encumbered elite positions in East Germany as well. Historian Sabrow: "Former Nazis here were of course subject to blackmail and played along all the more submissively in the anti-Fascist concert."

---

27. Reinhard Gehlen (1902-1979) was a major general in the German army and director of the division Foreign Armies East of the army's general staff. During the war, he was actively involved in the preparations for Operation Barbarossa, the attack on the Soviet Union in June 1941. With the faltering of the Russian campaign in 1942 the general staff looked for a new director of its army news service, which was in competition with the Reich Main Security Office. Although Gehlen had never been involved in secret service work, had not mastered a foreign language, and possessed no knowledge of the Soviet Union, he was appointed head of Foreign Armies East in May 1942 and was thereby also head of Nazi espionage in the East. He was also responsible for Scandinavia and southern Europe at first. Gehlen's methods for extracting information included brutal mass interrogations of prisoners of war in accordance with the motto of the Supreme Command of the army: "Any leniency or humaneness to prisoners of war is severely to be reprimanded." Following the defeat at Stalingrad in the winter of 1942-43, Gehlen worked closely with the SS Foreign Intelligence Service. A troop made up out of Soviet prisoners of war, deserters, and anti-communists was to be formed in the Soviet Union under General Vlassov, to act as a committee for the liberation of the peoples of Russia. It was Gehlen also who suggested "Operation Werwolf," a resistance group using underground weapons depots. From October 1944 on, Gehlen began planning for the time after the war, developing in the process a thesis that later turned out to be correct: "The Western powers will turn against their ally Russia. In doing this, they will need me, my co-workers, and my copied documents in the struggle against a communist expansion, because they have no agents of their own there." At the beginning of March 1945, a timely point before the end of the war, Gehlen had all the security documents copied on microfilm by hand-picked co-workers and, divided up among several mountain meadows, buried in the Austrian Alps. Beforehand, Gehlen had prepared their orderly transfer to the Americans with two of his top co-workers. On April 9, Hitler dismissed Gehlen, who left Army headquarters in Bad Reichenhall on April 28, went into hiding in a Bavarian alpine pasture near Miesbach, and surrendered, along with six officers, on May 22 to American soldiers in Fischhausen on the Schliersee. Gehlen was taken to Wiesbaden, where he was interrogated by Captain John Boker. As they talked it became clear that both had very similar visions of the role of the Americans in the future. The boxes hidden by Gehlen were dug up and taken to the document center in Frankfurt-Höchst. Captain Boker saw to it that several important colleagues of Gehlen's evaded arrest and imprisonment. Gehlen, now a prisoner of war for the time being, was flown at the order of the United States War Department to Fort Hunt, Virginia, with six former colleagues and the documents. As with Gehlen, the Allies took other experts into custody, including the rocket expert Wernher von Braun and nuclear physicists in the circle of Otto Hahn. Gehlen was later put in charge of the rebuilding of the West German Federal Intelligence Service; from 1956 to 1968 he was president of this.

1945 and 1946 – Further Consequences of the War in the German-Danish Region

The internment camp Frøslev on the German-Danish border played a special role as the war and the Nazi dictatorship came to an end. The camp was established in 1944 by the German occupation in the community of the same name just across the border in Danish territory and bore the name "Police Prison Camp Fröslee." The camp was mostly intended for political prisoners and Danish resistance fighters, and not for the detention an deportation of Jews. It was planned to hold 1,500 prisoners, but at the end of the war in April 1945 there were around 5,500 there. Danish organizations took care of food and medications for the prisoners, but they were forced to perform hard labor. Ultimately, the Nazis did not keep to their initial assurance that none of the prisoners would be sent to German concentration camps. Of the approximately 12,000 prisoners who passed through Camp Fröslee, at least 1,600 were sent via the nearby German railroad station in Harrislee to concentration camps, principally Hamburg-Neuengamme. A total of 220 of these were then murdered.

During the return of surviving Scandinavian concentration camp inmates as part of the rescue operation with Count Folke Bernadotte's White Buses in 1945, there was an intermediate stop in Fröslev.

Immediately after the end of the war in Denmark on May 5, 1945, the Danish resistance movement took charge. Members of the German minority were arrested and interned in the camp along with Danish collaborators. The control of the camp was then transferred to the state. For a time there were more than 5,500 prisoners in the camp, which had been renamed Faarhuslager, in order to put an end to the past days of Frøslevlager. Faarhus (sheep house) was the name of a neighboring village. In most cases, the detainees were charged with collaboration, but some were freed after a few weeks or months without having been charged. As a result of inadequate care by the Danish Red Cross, a few inmates died. The last were freed in October 1949.

"White Buses" was an operation undertaken by the Swedish Red Cross and the Danish government in the spring of 1945 to rescue concentration camp inmates.

2015 – A Wave of Refugees Surprises Germany

It's as if 70 years after the end of the war the Germans had something to "make good" to humanity: the first large-scale wave of immigration from the Near East and Africa reaches Europe and, especially, Germany. In the year 2015 alone, around 60 million people worldwide were fleeing their homeland. This is a number larger than ever before in the history of mankind. One-third of those fleeing war and poverty have left their home countries, while the remaining two-thirds are still on the move within their own borders. More than a million refugees were taken in by Germany in 2015 alone, mostly from Syria and Iraq.

On the one hand, people in Germany say "Welcome, refugees," while on the other, the social network threatens to fall apart. Growing criminality, an overburdened burocracy, a lack of integration due to organizational reasons—all these problems can gradually lead to reprehensible actions and to increasing dissatisfaction. There are already dangerous indications of a rapid strengthening of right-wing extremism. Added to this is a problem of particular concern: anti-Semitism among the refugees from the Arab world is very strong. Could a new and unusual alliance develop between right-wing extremist Germans (who are at this moment equally set against Muslims and Jews!) and anti-Jewish Arabs, in ways reminiscent of the Nazis' schemes to create enmities?

In any case, German politicians seem prepared to resist these beginnings, since before the seizure of power in 1933 there were similarly consequential tendencies in the people. At that time, extremists on the left and especially right-wing radical fanatics made the streets unsafe; the middle-class in the center said nothing or nurtured false hopes of security—until Hitler turned what he had previously announced into reality. And then it was all too late.

2015, Flensburg train station.

"Give me your tired, your poor, your huddled masses..."

In this booklet we have explored, among other things, some aspects of the Forty-Eighters, the democratic 1848er revolutionaries from Schleswig-Holstein who came to the United States seeking refuge from tyranny and who were successfully assimilated into American culture. It need hardly be pointed out how tragically different the fate of present-day refugees has been, especially those of Islamic background. Let us close now with a small ray of hope: the story of hundreds of refugees from the Middle East and how they were received at the railroad station in the far-northern German city of Flensburg on the Danish border. What follows is an abridged version of that story by Sabine Scholl, a teacher from that city.

On September 8, 2015, the media broadcast a report that caused many residents of Flensburg to pay a visit to what was usually our sleepy little railroad station: late in the evening, a great number of refugees had been unable to continue their trip to Scandinavia, since train traffic in that direction had been stopped. That evening I set out for the station along with others in hopes of being able to help. What I saw there I will never forget.

It seemed like a different world. The main concourse and the area in front of the station were full of countless people of many different nationalities. Old people, young men, families with little children were sitting everywhere as best they could, on spread-out blankets and pieces of cardboard. Some of them had dozed off. The whole place was filled with smoke and mist and a cacophony of different languages.

I asked a few individuals in English where they were from: Iraq, Afghanistan, Iran, Syria, Somalia, Eritrea. It suddenly seemed as if all the trouble spots of the world were right there. We had a sense of the horror and misery that had led these people to flee to Europe, and the dangers they had gone through on the way. Eventually I had to go home, wondering how they could possibly be given a place to stay overnight and what would happen to them afterwards.

The next day the waiting room looked completely chaotic. People were sleeping on the floor everywhere, on foam pads, on donated mattresses, on benches. In the middle of everything, mountains of clothing, cardboard boxes, packing material, empty bottles, and shoes. The air was sultry and smelled sour. A train arrived, bringing a torrent of commuters who had to plow their way through all the confusion. Office workers in shirts and ties, energetically hurrying to their work places, stood out in grotesque contrast to the scene in the waiting room. School children made their way around the sleeping figures, looking at the strange faces wide-eyed and in silence.

Around noon we suddenly heard an announcement: "In two hours a train will be arriving from Hamburg with over a hundred refugees." I swallowed hard. There were only two of us helpers left now, and not even a table or shelves where we could sort out the clothes. Gradually more people showed up to lend a hand. Then a class of future teachers from a girls' school came breezing in—what a blessing that was! From that point on everything went very smoothly. We improvised without much to work with, building shelves and tables out of cardboard boxes, painting signs, making piles of clothes. Soon the first refugees came streaming into the room and we helped them to find pants and winter jackets that fit them.

A variety of areas of responsibility gradually spread out in different parts of the station: a room with carefully sorted clothing, a personal hygiene corner (with razors, soap, diapers, and many more items), the food distribution table, and an information counter. An electrician made sure that we didn't have a power outage every time we plugged in an electric kettle. And suddenly there was even a refrigerator.

Temporary changing cubicles appeared, and a system of signs in many languages. On the internet portal of *Refugees Welcome in Flensburg* anyone could check to see what was needed currently—someone to do a job, language expertise, items of clothing or food—and then offer to help. More and more people willing to do their part threaded their way in, and along with them native speakers of Arabic, Pashto, and Persian, who became an essential part of the action group.

A Syrian who had lived in Flensburg for some time was the first interpreter. Using a megaphone, he passed on the most important information to the travelers in Arabic. For me and others, this was the first contact with that language. How beautiful and sonorous, how fiery, but also how dramatic it can sound! I hardly understood a single word, but it was my initial introduction to these people from the Arab world.

But Arabic was only one of the languages that you heard here. Whenever I stepped inside the building, the wave of language that hit me made me feel that I was entering a totally different world. A foreign language often creates a barrier, but it is also an invitation to find out by different means who the other person is, what he feels and what he needs. If there was no interpreter nearby, the only choice we had was to conduct dialogues "with hands and feet," or sometimes simply to offer a big smile. It was different at the information counter, though; there it was really important for people to make themselves understood, and in such cases knowledge of the language in question was essential.

Different people helped in different ways. An Afghani cook who works in a restaurant in Flensburg brought a pot of soup to the station after closing hours and personally filled bowls for the hungry people. "I came here in 2009. I still know how happy I would have been if someone had spoken to me in my language. That's what I want to do now for the people who come here."

Most of the first helpers of course were those who could take the time—housewives, retirees, and especially school children and university students. Later on I had the impression that a cross-section of our entire society had become actively involved. I got to know school children who loved doing their bit, often taking on unpleasant jobs like sorting old shoes. They came even though it wasn't always easy to deal with the things they were confronted with, since when they saw the refugees come streaming in from the trains, what they had heard about their misery suddenly became vivid and immediate. The anonymity that they had seen in the media melted away.

It was unbelievable, all the things that were brought to the station, whether homemade soup or mountains of longed-for fruits and vegetables. An older gentleman came in carrying a pair of pink children's shoes. "I bought these new. You see, I was a refugee myself, after the Second World War. I know what it's like not to have anything and not to know if anyone wants you around. Then I saw children here without any shoes. That's just not acceptable!"

For most of the helpers it was a matter of the heart to pass on as much warmth and cordiality as possible to the refugees, but also to create a sense of dignity, respect, and sympathy. Many people's expressions brightened up with surprise when a friendly German helper could say the Arabic words for bread, olives, and tea. There were certainly unpleasant encounters involving refugees as well. More than once, someone stood before me whom I would have preferred not to help, since I was greeted with the opposite of friendliness. But at the same time I thought: Do you only want to help when it's easy? Do you only want to help people you think are pleasant? What is important is offering help because the situation demands it, because this person, no matter how I feel about him, is a person in distress.

Appendix 1: Speech by Richard von Weizsäcker   73
       "All of us must accept the past"

Appendix 2: Holocaust Education in the 21st Century   83
       A Flensburg Perspective: Erna de Vries and the Holocaust Boxcar (a video)

Appendix 3: The Legacy of 1848   87
       Transplanted Ideas & Values in America's Past and Present

Appendix 1
Speech by Richard von Weizsäcker

"All of us must accept the past"

"It was deathly quiet in Parliament on May 8, 1985 as Federal President Richard v. Weizsäcker (Bonn, West Germany) gave his speech memorializing the end of the Second World War. This, in any case, was how the *New York Times* described the atmosphere, seeing in the address above all the demand that the German people accept its past. The Israeli ambassador at the time, Yitzhak Ben Ari, a guest in the visitors' gallery, heard words which "in their sober, precise quality rendered the incomprehensible comprehensible." Weizsäcker's address, speaking to and deeply moving "all the victims and those ensnared by feelings of guilt," was, he said, "a high point in the history of the Federal Republic." The deluge of letters and the record-breaking dissemination of the manuscript, two million copies of which were printed with translations in thirteen different languages—these numbers themselves give an impression of the positive response to the speech, which is considered today a major cultural turning point."

Bonn, capital of West Germany, May 8th, 1985, Richard von Weizsäcker in the German Parliament.

Speech by President Richard von Weizsäcker during the Ceremony Commemorating the 40th Anniversary of the End of War in Europe and of National-Socialist Tyranny on 8 May 1985 at the Bundestag, Bonn:

I.

Many nations are today commemorating the date on which World War II ended in Europe. Every nation is doing so with different feelings, depending on its fate. Be it victory or defeat, liberation from injustice and alien rule or transition to new dependence, division, new alliances, vast shifts of power – 8 May 1945 is a date of decisive historical importance for Europe.

We Germans are commemorating that date amongst ourselves, as is indeed necessary. We must find our own standards. We are not assisted in this task if we or others spare our feelings. We need and we have the strength to look truth straight in the eye – without embellishment and without distortion.

For us, the 8th of May is above all a date to remember what people had to suffer. It is also a date to reflect on the course taken by our history. The greater honesty we show in commemorating this day, the freer we are to face the consequences with due responsibility. For us Germans, 8 May is not a day of celebration. Those who actually witnessed that day in 1945 think back on highly personal and hence highly different experiences. Some returned home, others lost their homes. Some were liberated, whilst for others it was the start of captivity. Many were simply grateful that the bombing at night and fear had passed and that they had survived. Others felt first and foremost grief at the complete defeat suffered by their country. Some Germans felt bitterness about their shattered illusions, whilst others were grateful for the gift of a new start.

It was difficult to find one's bearings straight away. Uncertainty prevailed throughout the country. The military capitulation was unconditional, placing our destiny in the hands of our enemies. The past had been terrible, especially for many of those enemies, too. Would they not make us pay many times over for what we had done to them? Most Germans had believed that they were fighting and suffering for the good of their country. And now it turned out that their efforts were not only in vain and futile, but had served the inhuman goals of a criminal regime. The feelings of most people were those of exhaustion, despair and new anxiety. Had one's next of kin survived? Did a new start from those ruins make sense at all? Looking back, they saw the dark abyss of the past and, looking forward, they saw an uncertain, dark future.

Yet with every day something became clearer, and this must be stated on behalf of all of us today: the 8th of May was a day of liberation. It liberated all of us from the inhumanity and tyranny of the National-Socialist regime.

Nobody will, because of that liberation, forget the grave suffering that only started for many people on 8 May. But we must not regard the end of the war as the cause of flight, expulsion and deprivation of freedom. The cause goes back to the start of the tyranny that brought about war. We must not separate 8 May 1945 from 30 January 1933.

There is truly no reason for us today to participate in victory celebrations. But there is every reason for us to perceive 8 May 1945 as the end of an aberration in German history, an end bearing seeds of hope for a better future.

II.

8 May is a day of remembrance. Remembering means recalling an occurrence honestly and undistortedly so that it becomes a part of our very beings. This places high demands on our truthfulness.

Today we mourn all the dead of the war and the tyranny. In particular we commemorate the six million Jews who were murdered in German concentration camps. We commemorate all nations who suffered in the war, especially the countless citizens of the Soviet Union and Poland who lost their lives. As Germans, we mourn our own compatriots who perished as soldiers, during air raids at home, in captivity or during expulsion. We commemorate the Sinti and Romany gypsies, the homosexuals and the mentally ill who were killed, as well as the people who had to die for their religious or political beliefs. We commemorate the hostages who were executed. We recall the victims of the resistance movements in all the countries occupied by us. As Germans, we pay homage to the victims of the German resistance – among the public, the military, the churches, the workers and trade unions, and the communists. We commemorate those who did not actively resist, but preferred to die instead of violating their consciences.

Alongside the endless army of the dead, mountains of human suffering arise – grief at the dead, suffering from injury or crippling or barbarous compulsory sterilization, suffering during the air raids, during flight and expulsion, suffering because of rape and pillage, forced labour, injustice and torture, hunger and hardship, suffering because of fear of arrest and death, grief at the loss of everything which one had wrongly believed in and worked for. Today we sorrowfully recall all this human suffering.

Perhaps the greatest burden was borne by the women of all nations. Their suffering, renunciation and silent strength are all too easily forgotten by history. Filled with fear, they worked, bore human life and protected it. They mourned their fallen fathers and sons, husbands, brothers and friends. In the years of darkness, they ensured that the light of humanity was not extinguished. After the war, with no prospect of a secure future, women everywhere were the first to set about building homes again, the "rubble women" in Berlin and elsewhere. When the men who had survived returned, women often had to take a back seat again. Because of the war, many women were left alone and spent their lives in solitude. Yet it is first and foremost thanks to the women that nations did not disintegrate spiritually on account of the destruction, devastation, atrocities and inhumanity and that they gradually regained their foothold after the war.

III.

At the root of the tyranny was Hitler's immeasurable hatred against our Jewish compatriots. Hitler had never concealed this hatred from the public, but made the entire nation a tool of it. Only a day before his death, on 30 April 1945, he concluded his so-called will with the words: "Above all, I call upon the leaders of the nation and their followers to observe painstakingly the race laws and to oppose ruthlessly the poisoners of all nations: international Jewry." It is true that hardly any country has in its history always remained free from blame for war or violence. The genocide of the Jews is, however, unparalleled in history.

The perpetration of this crime was in the hands of a few people. It was concealed from the eyes of the public, but every German was able to witness what his Jewish compatriots had to suffer, ranging from plain apathy and hidden intolerance to outright hatred. Who could remain unsuspecting after the burning of the synagogues, the plundering, the stigmatization with the Star of David, the deprivation of rights, the ceaseless violation of human dignity? Whoever opened his eyes and ears and sought information could not fail to notice that Jews were being deported. The nature and scope of the destruction may have exceeded human imagination, but in reality there was, apart from the crime itself, the attempt by too many people, including those of my generation, who were young and were not involved in planning the events and carrying them out, not to take note of what was happening. There were many ways of not burdening one's conscience, of shunning responsibility, looking away, keeping mum. When the unspeakable truth of the Holocaust then became known at the end of the war, all too many of us claimed that they had not known anything about it or even suspected anything.

There is no such thing as the guilt or innocence of an entire nation. Guilt is, like innocence, not collective, but personal. There is discovered or concealed individual guilt. There is guilt which people acknowledge or deny. Everyone who directly experienced that era should today quietly ask himself about his involvement then.

The vast majority of today's population were either children then or had not been born. They cannot profess a guilt of their own for crimes that they did not commit. No discerning person can expect them to wear a penitential robe simply because they are Germans. But their forefathers have left them a grave legacy. All of us, whether guilty or not, whether old or young, must accept the past. We are all affected by its consequences and liable for it. The young and old generations must and can help each other to understand why it is vital to keep alive the memories. It is not a case of coming to terms with the past. That is not possible. It cannot be subsequently modified or made undone. However, anyone who closes his eyes to the past is blind to the present. Whoever refuses to remember the inhumanity is prone to new risks of infection.

The Jewish nation remembers and will always remember. We seek reconciliation as human beings. Precisely for this reason we must understand that there can be no reconciliation without remembrance. The experience of millionfold death is part of the very being of every Jew in the world, not only because people cannot forget such atrocities, but also because remembrance is part of the Jewish faith.

"Seeking to forget makes exile all the longer; the secret of redemption lies in remembrance?" This oft quoted Jewish adage surely expresses the idea that faith in God is faith in the work of God in history. Remembrance is experience of the work of God in history. It is the source of faith in redemption. This experience creates hope, it creates faith in redemption, in reunification of the divided, in reconciliation. Whoever forgets this experience loses his faith.

If we for our part sought to forget what has occurred, instead of remembering it, this would not only be inhuman. We would also impinge upon the faith of the Jews who survived and destroy the basis of reconciliation. We must erect a memorial to thoughts and feelings in our own hearts.

IV.

The 8th of May marks a deep cut not only in German history but in the history of Europe as a whole. The European civil war had come to an end, the old world of Europe lay in ruins. "Europe had fought itself to a standstill" (M. Stürmer). The meeting of American and Soviet Russian soldiers on the Elbe became a symbol for the temporary end of a European era.

True, all this was deeply rooted in history. The Europeans had a great, indeed dominating influence in the world, but they were less and less capable of maintaining orderly relations among themselves on their own continent. For more than a century Europe had suffered under the clash of extreme nationalistic aspirations. At the end of the First World War peace treaties were signed but they lacked the power to foster peace. Once more nationalistic passions flared up and were fanned by the distress of the people at that time.

Along the road to disaster Hitler became the driving force. He whipped up and exploited mass hysteria. A weak democracy was incapable of stopping him. And even the powers of Western Europe – in Churchill's judgment unsuspecting but not without guilt – contributed through their weakness to this fateful trend. After the First World War America had withdrawn and in the thirties had no influence on Europe.

Hitler wanted to dominate Europe and to do so through war. He looked for and found an excuse in Poland. On 23 May 1939 – only a few months before the Outbreak of war – he told the German generals: "No further successes can be gained without bloodshed ... Danzig is not the objective. Our aim is to extend our Lebensraum in the East and safeguard food supplies ... So there is no question of sparing Poland; and there remains the decision to attack Poland at the first suitable opportunity ... In this context, neither right nor wrong nor treaties matter?"

On 23 August 1939 Germany and the Soviet Union signed a non-aggression pact. The secret supplementary protocol made provision for the impending partition of Poland. That pact was made to give Hitler an opportunity to invade Poland. The Soviet leaders at the time were fully aware of this. And all who understood politics realized that the implications of the German-Soviet pact were Hitler's invasion of Poland and hence the Second World War.

That does not mitigate Germany's responsibility for the outbreak of the Second World War. The Soviet Union was prepared to allow other nations to fight one another so that it could have a share of the spoils. The initiative for the war, however, came from Germany, not from the Soviet Union. It was Hitler who resorted to the use of force.

The outbreak of the Second World War remains linked with the name of Germany.

In the course of that war the Nazi regime tormented and defiled many nations. At the end of it all only one nation remained to be tormented, enslaved and defiled: its own, the German nation. Time and again Hitler had declared that if the German nation was not capable of winning the war it should be left to perish. The other nations first became victims of a war started by Germany before we became the victims of our own war.

There followed the division of Germany into zones as agreed among the victorious powers. In the meantime the Soviet Union had taken control in all countries of Eastern and South-eastern Europe that had been occupied by Germany during the war. All of them, with the exception of Greece, became socialist states. The division of Europe into two different political systems took its course. True, it was the post-war developments which cemented that division, but without the war started by Hitler it would not have happened at all. That is what first comes to the minds of the nations concerned when they recall the war unleashed by the German leaders. And we think of that too when we ponder the division of our own country and the loss of huge sections of German territory. In a sermon in East Berlin commemorating the 8th of May, Cardinal Meißner said: "The pathetic result of sin is always division?"

V.

The arbitrariness of destruction continued to be felt in the arbitrary distribution of burdens. There were innocent people who were persecuted and guilty ones who got away. Some were lucky to be able to begin life all over again at home in familiar surroundings. Others were expelled from the lands of their fathers. We in what was to become the Federal Republic of Germany were given the priceless opportunity to live in freedom. Many millions of our countrymen have been denied that opportunity to this day.

Learning to accept mentally this arbitrary allocation of fate was the first task, alongside the material task of rebuilding the country. That had to be the test of the human strength to recognize the burdens of others, to help bear them over time, not to forget them. It had to be the test of our ability to work for peace, of our willingness to foster the spirit of reconciliation both at home and in our external relations, an ability and a readiness which not only others expected of us but which we most of all demanded of ourselves.

We cannot commemorate the 8th of May without being conscious of the great effort required on the part of our former enemies to set out on the road of reconciliation with us. Can we really place ourselves in the position of relatives of the victims of the Warsaw ghetto or of the

Lidice massacre? And how hard must it have been for the citizens of Rotterdam or London to support the rebuilding of our country from where the bombs came which not long before had been dropped on their cities? To be able to do so they had gradually to gain the assurance that the Germans would not again try to make good their defeat by use of force.

In our country the biggest sacrifice was demanded of those who had been driven out of their homeland. They were to experience great suffering and grievous injustice long after the 8th of May. Those of us who were born here often do not have the imagination nor the open heart with which to grasp the real meaning of their harsh fate.

But soon there were great signs of readiness to help. Many millions of refugees and expellees were taken in who over the years were able to strike new roots. Their children and grandchildren have in many different ways formed a loving attachment to the culture and the homeland of their ancestors. Well that they have, for that is a great treasure in their lives. But they themselves have found a new home where they are growing up and integrating with the local people of the same age, sharing their dialect and their customs. Their young life is proof of their ability to be at peace with themselves. Their grandparents or parents were once driven out; they themselves, however, are now at home.

Very soon and in exemplary fashion the expellees identified themselves with the renunciation of force. That was no passing declaration in the early stages of helplessness but a commitment which has retained its validity. Renouncing the use of force means allowing trust to grow on all sides; it means that a Germany that has regained its strength remains bound by it. The expellees' own homeland has meanwhile become a homeland for others. In many of the old cemeteries in Eastern Europe you will today find more Polish than German graves. The compulsory migration of millions of Germans to the West was followed by the migration of millions of Poles and, in their wake, millions of Russians. These are all people who were not asked, people who suffered injustice, people who became defenceless objects of political events and to whom no compensation for those injustices and no offsetting of claims can make up for what has been done to them.

Renouncing force today means giving them lasting security, unchallenged on political grounds, for their future in the place where fate drove them after the 8th of May and were they have been living in the decades since. It means placing the dictate of understanding above conflicting legal claims. That is the true, the human contribution to a peaceful order in Europe which we can provide.

The new beginning in Europe after 1945 has brought both victory and defeat for the notion of freedom and self-determination. Our aim is to seize the opportunity to draw a line under a long period of European history in which to every country peace seemed conceivable and safe only as a result of its own supremacy, and in which peace meant a period of preparation for the next war.

The nations of Europe love their homeland. The Germans are no different. Who could trust in a nation's love of peace if it were capable of forgetting its homeland? No, love of peace manifests itself precisely in the fact that one does not forget one's homeland and is for that very reason resolved to do everything in one's power to live together with others in lasting peace. An expellee's love for his homeland is in no way revanchism.

VI.

The last war has aroused a stronger desire for peace in the hearts of men than in times past. The work of the churches in promoting reconciliation met with a tremendous response. There are many examples of practical efforts by young people to promote understanding. One is the "Aktion Sühnezeichen", a campaign concentrating on atonement activity in Auschwitz and Israel. Recently, a parish in the town of Kleve on the lower Rhine received loaves of bread from Polish parishes as a token of reconciliation and fellowship. It sent one of those loaves to a teacher in England because he had discarded his anonymity and written to say that as a member of a bomber crew during the war he had destroyed the church and houses in Kleve and wanted to take part in some gesture of reconciliation. In seeking peace it is a tremendous help if, instead of waiting for the other to come to us, we go towards him, as this man did.

VII.

In the wake of the war, old enemies were brought closer together both as human beings and politically. As early as 1946, the American Secretary of State, James F. Byrnes, called in his memorable Stuttgart address for understanding in Europe and for assistance to the German nation on its way to a free and peaceable future. Innumerable Americans assisted us Germans, who had lost the war, with their own private means so as to heal the wounds of war. Thanks to the vision of Frenchmen like Jean Monnet and Robert Schuman and of Germans like Konrad Adenauer, the traditional enmity between the French and Germans was buried forever.

A new will and energy to reconstruct Germany surged through the country. Many an old trench was filled in, religious differences and social strains were defused. People set to work in a spirit of partnership. There was no "zero hour", but we had the opportunity to make a fresh start. We have used this opportunity as well as we could.

We have put democratic freedom in the place of oppression. Four years after the end of the war, on this 8th of May in 1949, the Parliamentary Council adopted our Basic Law. Transcending party differences, the democrats on the Council gave their answer to war and tyranny in Article 1 of our Constitution: "The German people therefore acknowledge inviolable and inalienable human rights as the basis of any community, of peace and of justice in the world." This further significance of 8 May should also be remembered today.

The Federal Republic of Germany has become an internationally respected State. It is one of the most highly developed industrial countries in the world. It knows that its economic strength commits it to share responsibility for the struggle against hunger and need in the world and for social adjustment between nations. For 40 years we have been living in peace and freedom, to which we, through our policy in union with the free nations of the Atlantic Alliance and the European Community, have ourselves rendered a major contribution. The freedom of the individual has never received better protection in Germany than it does today. A comprehensive system of social welfare that can stand comparison with any other ensures the subsistence of the population. Whereas at the end of the war many Germans tried to hide their passports or to exchange them for another one, German nationality today is highly valued.

We certainly have no reason to be arrogant and self-righteous. But we may look back with gratitude on our development over these 40 years, if we use the memory of our own history as a guideline for our behaviour now and in tackling the unresolved problems that lie ahead.

If we remember that mentally disturbed persons were put to death in the Third Reich, we will see care of people with psychiatric disorders as our own responsibility.

If we remember how people persecuted on grounds of race, religion and politics and threatened with certain death often stood before the closed borders with other countries, we shall not close the door today on those who are genuinely persecuted and seek protection with us.

If we reflect on the penalties for free thinking under the dictatorship, we will protect the freedom of every idea and every criticism, however much it may be directed against ourselves.

Whoever criticizes the situation in the Middle East should think of the fate to which Germans condemned their Jewish fellow human beings, a fate that led to the establishment of the State of Israel under conditions which continue to burden and pose a danger to people in that region even today.

If we think of what our Eastern neighbours had to suffer during the war, we will find it easier to understand that accommodation, detente and peaceful neighbourly relations with these countries remain central tasks of German foreign policy. It is important that both sides remember and that both sides respect each other. They have every reason to on human, on cultural and in the final analysis on historical grounds also. Mikhail Gorbachov, General Secretary of the Soviet Communist Party, declared that it was not the intention of the Soviet leaders at the 40th anniversary of the end of the war to stir up anti-German feelings. The Soviet Union, he said, was committed to friendship between nations. Particularly if we have doubts about Soviet contributions to understanding between East and West and about respect for human rights in all parts of Europe, we must not ignore this signal from Moscow. We seek friendship with the peoples of the Soviet Union.

VIII.

Forty years after the end of the war, the German nation remains divided.

At a commemorative service in the Church of the Holy Cross in Dresden held in February of this year, Bishop Hempel said: "It is a burden and a scourge that two German States have emerged with their harsh border. The very multitude of borders is a burden and a scourge. Weapons are a burden."

Recently in Baltimore in the United States, an exhibition on "Jews in Germany" was opened. The Ambassadors of both German States accepted the invitation to attend. The host, the President of the Johns Hopkins University, welcomed them together. He stated that all Germans share the same historical development. Their joint past is a bond that links them. Such a bond, he said, could be a blessing or a problem, but was always a source of hope.

We Germans are one people and one nation. We feel that we belong together because we have lived through the same past. We also experienced the 8th of May 1945 as part of the common fate of our nation, which unites us. We feel bound together in our desire for peace. Peace and good neighbourly relations with all countries should radiate from the German soil in both States. And no other states should let that soil become a source of danger to peace either. The people of Germany are united in desiring a peace that encompasses justice and human rights for all peoples, including our own. Reconciliation that transcends boundaries cannot be provided by a walled Europe but only by a continent that removes the divisive elements from its borders. That is the exhortation given us by the end of the Second World War. We are confident that the 8th of May is not the last date in the common history of all Germans.

IX.

Many young people have in recent months asked themselves and us why such animated discussions about the past have arisen 40 years after the end of the war. Why are they more animated than after 25 or 30 years? What is the inherent necessity of this development?

It is not easy to answer such questions. But we should not seek the reasons primarily in external influences, though they doubtlessly existed. In the life-span of men and in the destiny of nations, 40 years play a great role. Permit me at this point to return again to the Old Testament, which contains deep insights for every person, irrespective of his own faith. There 40 years frequently play a vital part. The Israelites were to remain in the desert for 40 years before a new stage in their history began with their arrival in the promised land. Forty years were required for a complete transfer of responsibility from the generation of the fathers.

Yet elsewhere (in the Book of Judges) it is described how often the memory of experienced assistance and rescue lasted only for 40 years. When that memory faded, tranquility was at an end. Forty years thus invariably constitute a significant time-span. Man perceives them as the end of a dark age bringing hope for a new and prosperous future, or as the onset of danger that the past might be forgotten and as a warning of the consequences. It is worth reflecting on both of these perceptions.

In our country, a new generation has grown up to assume political responsibility. Our young people are not responsible for what happened over forty years ago. But they are responsible for the historical consequences.

We in the older generation owe to young people not the fulfilment of dreams but honesty. We must help younger people to understand why it is vital to keep memories alive. We want to help them to accept historical truth soberly, not one-sidedly, without taking refuge in utopian doctrines, but also without moral arrogance. From our own history we learn what man is capable of. For that reason we must not imagine that we are now quite different and have become better. There is no ultimately achievable moral perfection – for no individual and for no nation. We have learned as human beings, and as human beings we remain in danger. But we have the strength to overcome such danger again and again.

Hitler's constant approach was to stir up prejudices, enmity and hatred. What is asked of young people today is this: do not let yourselves be forced into enmity and hatred of other people, of Russians or Americans, Jews or Turks, of alternatives or conservatives, blacks or whites. Learn to live together, not in opposition to each other.

As democratically elected politicians, we, too, should heed this time and again and set a good example.

Let us honour freedom.

Let us work for peace.

Let us respect the rule of law.

Let us be true to our own conception of justice.

On this 8th of May, let us face up as well as we can to the truth.

Katrin Hammerstein, Birgit Hofmann, "Wir […] müssen die Vergangenheit annehmen" – Richard von Weizsäckers Rede zum Kriegsende 1985, in: Deutschland Archiv, 18.12.2015, Link: www.bpb.de/217619

www.bpb.de/geschichte/zeitgeschichte/deutschlandarchiv/217619/richard-von-weizsaeckers-rede-zum-kriegsende-1985 (Federal Agency for Civic Education / Bundeszentrale für politische Bildung, Bonn, Germany.)

Appendix 2
Holocaust Education in the 21st Century

A Flensburg Perspective: Erna de Vries and the Holocaust Boxcar (a video)

In 2015 my wife Gitta Reppmann and I organized the transportation of what can be called a "Holocaust boxcar" from a forest in central Germany to the impressive Fagen Fighters World War II Museum in Granite Falls, Minnesota, where it is now on display. On January 12, 2017, the Auschwitz survivor Erna de Vries, age 93, was featured in the filming of an "Untold Story" in the city of Flensburg. Integral to the background of the story is the fact—certainly unknown to most Americans—that in the final days of the war hundreds of high-ranking Nazis went into hiding in this city, which briefly became a sort of new "capital of the Reich."

Erna de Vries, Lathen, Germany.

How the story of the boxcar in the Fagen Fighters Museum ends:

The story of the boxcar is inseparably connected with the history of the Nazi death camps. Erna de Vries (née Korn), a Holocaust survivor, makes a journey through time more than seventy years after her liberation. Once again she is sitting in a train, just as she was at the time she was taken to Auschwitz in an ordinary railroad passenger car. Memories of that journey, on the way to the intended annihilation of the Jews at the hands of the Nazis, resurge in her mind.

Now she wants to see and feel how the perpetrators, who considered themselves members of the master race, showed their true colors at the end of the war. Three days before the surrender on May 8, 1945, several of the mass murderers, among them SS Reichsführer Heinrich Himmler, Auschwitz Commandant Rudolf Höß, and the Chief Inspector of Concentration Camps Richard Glücks, met at police headquarters in Flensburg. At this meeting the contempt of these war criminals for mankind was no longer the point, but only how they could go into hiding. Their last stop was a flight from responsibility.

Seventy-one years after this meeting, Erna de Vries sits in this room for the first time, remembering her own path of suffering in the very same location where the perpetrators of these crimes were unmasked one final time as unscrupulous criminals.

With the arrest of the final official state government on May 23, this town now becomes the last stop for the entire band of Nazis. The Auschwitz survivor looks at the cells in the building, experiences once again her liberation and the end of both the Second World War and the Nazi top brass.

With her visit to the town where one final scene was played out following the surrender, the circle is closed. She has survived and can now set out to tell subsequent generations about the Holocaust and the cowardly murderers who perpetrated it.

A television documentation of this unusual complex of events in Flensburg during the final days of the war, was produced in March 2017 by Stephan Witthöft, Erfurt, SALVE MEDIA; *A Flensburg Perspective: Erna de Vries and the Holocaust Boxcar.*
(www.Moin-Moin.us 'Videos')

Erinnerung an zwei „48er"

Christian-Albrechts-Universität ehrt die Brüder Theodor und Justus Olshausen mit einer eigenen

Kiel – Obwohl die Olshausenstraße gewissermaßen die Central Avenue der Universität darstellt, lässt sich heute nicht mehr rekonstruieren, ob ihr Name auf Theodor oder seinen Bruder Justus Olshausen Bezug nimmt. Als Vorkämpfer der Demokratie während der 1848er Revolution hätten beide es verdient – weshalb ihnen die Alma Mater nun eine eigene Gedenkstele widmet.

Von Oliver Stenzel

Der eine war ein bedeutender Gelehrter, der andere ein umtriebiger Journalist und Verleger. Gemeinsam war Justus und Theodor Olshausen ihr engagiertes Eintreten für die Demokratie in der Mitte des 19. Jahrhunderts. Während der Kieler Orientalistik-Professor Justus 1848 nicht nur

Kieler Nachrichten (Kiel Daily Newspaper) June 6, 2009, reporting about a new Theodore and Justus Olshausen 1848er memorial installation, located on Olshausenstrasse, the main street that runs through the Kiel university campus in the State of Schleswig-Holstein. Professor Fouquet, University President, Yogi Reppmann, event manager, and Cathy Kietzer, Kiel City President.

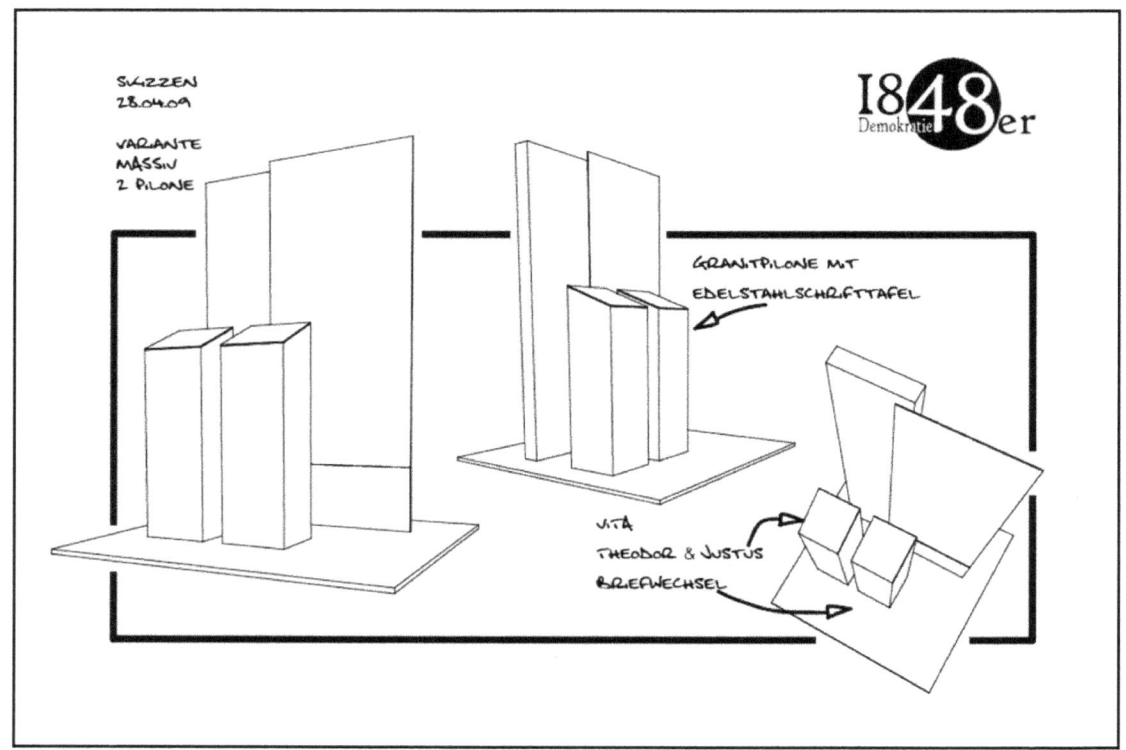

Drawing of the Forty-Eighter Memorial Installation.

Appendix 3
The Legacy of 1848:

Transplanted Ideas & Values in America's Past and Present

The "Forty-Eighters" were a relatively small number of individuals who left Germany in the late 1840s and early 1850s after fighting unsuccessfully with both pen and sword for liberty, democracy, and national unity. Many of these courageous men emigrated to the United States. A large number from the present-day state of Schleswig-Holstein chose Davenport and Scott County, Iowa, on the Mississippi River, as their adopted home. After settling in America, these talented individuals provided an intellectual transfusion for their newly-founded German-American communities, while also influencing the political and social history of the United States during one of its most critical periods.

Memorial Installations for Gabriel Riesser?

In an attempt to highlight these outstanding Forty-Eighters' contributions, we would like to see a monument for GabrielRiesser and Theodore Olshausen in Davenport and in the City of Lauenburg, Schleswig-Holstein, and/or Hamburg.

In 1848 Riesser (2 April 1806 - 22 April 1863) was a member of the democratic revolutionary *Frankfurt Parliament/St. Paul's Church* where he was a vice-president. He was elected for the constituency of Saxe-Lauenburg, northeast of Hamburg. Riesser was a member of the *Kaiserdeputation* which offered the Prussian King Frederick Wilhelm IV the German crown. When the civil rights of the *Paulskirchenverfassung* (Constitution of 1848) came into effect, Riesser was able to become a citizen of Hamburg, a rare and valued franchise at the time. In 1856 he traveled to Davenport, Iowa to visit his close friend Theodore Olshausen, a leading 1848er in Schleswig-Holstein and America. In 1860 he became the first Jewish judge in Germany.

Many of the Forty-Eighters left lasting marks in politics, education, business, journalism, the arts, and the military. Carl Schurz, perhaps the best-known of those who settled in America, achieved great success in no less than four of these areas. During his long and illustrious career, he was ambassador to Spain for President Lincoln, a general during the Civil War, a United States senator, and Secretary of the Interior under President Rutherford B. Hayes. Carl Schurz served as a leading journalist of the *Westliche Post* in St. Louis, the *New York Evening Post*, and editorial writer for *Harper's Weekly*.

The legacy of Carl Schurz is especially timely today. With the steady increase of immigration to the United States and the ongoing refugee crisis in Germany, it has become ever more important to establish the proper framework for the absorption and integration of newcomers. Schurz's solution – assimilation while retaining the newcomers' ethnic heritage – is as valid today as it was when he articulated it in the nineteenth century. The fusion of ethnic identities and American / German values is of the greatest importance, and Carl Schurz's life is a worthy paradigm for all immigrants to emulate.

Most Europeans and Americans know little if anything of the extensive and extremely significant legacy of the Forty-Eighters.

Wolfgang Börnsen and Dr. Henry Kissinger

Wolfgang Börnsen (second from left), long-time member of the German Parliament, March 18, 2012, in Berlin, on the "Platz des 18. März" (behind the Brandenburg Gate). Börnsen motivated a bipartisan group of colleagues to suggest 'March 18th' as a federal day of remembrance. (In memory of the "Barrikadenkämpfe", on March 18th and 19th, 1848, students, citizens, and laborers joined together in Berlin to defeat the Prussian army in the democratic revolution of 1848.)

"1999, Yogi and a student of his pose for a picture with former U.S. Secretary of State Dr. Henry Kissinger in his New York office.

Yogi was first introduced to Kissinger by Gerhard Stoltenberg, a fatherly friend to both Yogi ad Dee Eicke. Stoltenberg, who served as Governor of Schleswig-Holstein, first met Kissinger when he was teaching at Harvard in 1953, and the two historians established a close friendship. In December of 1999, Yogi was present at a book party given by his newspaper editor friend, Stephan Richter, who had just published what proved to be Stoltenberg's last book. During this party, a video shot by Yogi with Kissinger's greetings from New York caused tears to well up in the eyes of the old politician. - Yogi loves to tell his Kissinger marzipan story. At the end of his meeting with the great man in 1999, Yogi presented him with a gift of Lübeck's finest marzipan. Kissinger, who had been little standoffish prior to that moment, left the room, returned visibly moved, and asked 'How did you know?' Unbeknownst to Yogi, Lübeck marzipan was a very fond childhood memory for Kissinger. He related how only once a year — at the time before Christmas — could his parents in Germany afford to buy the world's best marzipan, Lübeck marzipan. - Every time Yogi returns to New York, he always stops by Kissinger's office and brings him some marzipan, or if not in the country, mails him some before Christmas. Unfailingly, Kissinger responds with a sweet letter." In: Scott C. Christiansen, „Soul of Schleswig-Holstein", p. 148*. (fascinating coffee table book: Printing on Demand, www.Lulu.com).

"Dear Yogi, Congratulations on the re-dedication of the monument to the Schleswig-Holsteiners who came to Davenport in 1848-1850 to escape the oppressive conditions in their homeland. Their descendants and others of German stock who arrived in America in the mid-19th century have been one of America's most successful immigrant groups. They deserve this monument, … Thank you for the marzipan. I have no better source for the real thing, but can always count on you! … I hope you will have a most enjoyable summer in Flensburg., Warm Regards, [signed] *Henry Kissinger*" (letter from April 30, 2008) … I read the booklet that you co-wrote with Friedhelm Caspari, *The Holocaust Boxcar—A Powerful Admonition Against Anti-Semitism,* with interest, and look forward to the updates you send on the German-American Forty-Eighters. Congratulations on all of the good work you do. [signed] Sincerely, *Henry. A. Kissinger"* (letter from November 3, 2016)

*T*he Soul of Schleswig-Holstein: An Iowan's Insight into His Ancestral Homeland, Scott C. Christiansen, Up Ewig Ungedeelt Press, Iowa City, Iowa, 2009.

In this fascinating history, Christiansen explores not only his immigrant ancestor, but also the Forty-Eighters and their importance for Germany and America, placing his work in the context of an in-depth portrait of Schleswig-Holstein. Richly illustrated with almost eight hundred colored photographs and maps and with a detailed index (pp. 239-283), this coffee table book clearly demonstrates the significance of the Forty-Eighters, as well as the importance of Schleswig-Holstein for the history of the German immigration to America, especially for the state of Iowa. A beautifully written work, Christiansen also presents a perceptive exploration of the values of the German Forty-Eighters and their relevance for today. Available from: www.LuLu.com (Printing on Demand).

Don Heinrich Tolzmann, Book Review Editor, in: German Life, November/December 2009.

For more information, see the moving educational video "Forty-Eighters and Friends," which highlights the lives and achievements of Davenport's Forty-Eighters from Schleswig-Holstein: www.Moin-Moin.us (Menu 'Videos-English')

Carl Schurz Monument in Berlin?

In the spring of 2016, an influential German weekly news source published an valuable article about the legacy of 1848 and the German Forty-Eighters in America:

DER SPIEGEL (Dirk Kurbjuweit) inspired the German Federal President, Dr. Frank-Walter Steinmeier, to support the creation of a Forty-Eighter Monument. The article suggests the monument be placed in Berlin.

Hecker

Sigel

Struve

Schurz

ERINNERUNG
Steinmeier und die Forty-Eighters

Bundesaußenminister Frank-Walter Steinmeier unterstützt die Idee, den sogenannten Forty-Eighters ein Denkmal zu errichten. Es geht dabei um frühe deutsche Demokraten wie Carl Schurz, Friedrich Hecker, Gustav Struve und Franz Sigel, die an der gescheiterten Revolution von 1848/49 beteiligt waren. Sie emigrierten danach in die USA und kämpften im Bürgerkrieg gegen die Sklavenhalterei. Steinmeier: „Im historischen Gedächtnis vieler Menschen haben die Amerikaner, unterstützt von den Briten und Franzosen, 1945 die Demokratie nach Deutschland gebracht. Dabei gab es aber schon vor 1933 eine parlamentarische Erfahrungsbasis, die von den Akteuren 1848 hart erkämpft wurde. Deshalb ist das Denkmal für die sogenannten Forty-Eighters eine große Chance, an die wechselseitige Einflussnahme beim Aufbau stabiler Demokratien auf beiden Seiten des Ozeans zu erinnern." Den Vorschlag für ein solches Denkmal in der Hauptstadt hatte der SPIEGEL in der AUSGABE 14/2016 gemacht. Unter den Unterstützern, die sich daraufhin meldeten, sind der Schauspieler Ulrich Matthes und Erardo Cristoforo Rautenberg, der Generalstaatsanwalt von Brandenburg. Rautenberg hat bereits ein Konzept für eine Erinnerungsstätte entwickelt. In den USA gibt es mehrere Denkmäler für Carl Schurz, der es dort bis zum Senator und Innenminister gebracht hat. Rautenberg schlägt vor, eine dieser amerikanischen Büsten zu kopieren und in Berlin auf einen Sockel zu stellen. Eine Tafel solle an andere bekannte Forty-Eighters erinnern. dk

Der Spiegel, April 23rd, 2016.
Detailed information: www.moin-moin.us

Highlights: Northfield Conference 2017

Holocaust Education and the Legacy of 1848

On April 1, Consul General Herbert Quelle presented Dr. Joachim "Yogi" Reppmann with the *German American Friendship Award*. The Prize, established in 1981, is given by the German Ambassador to those who have shown extraordinary commitment to fostering German-American relations.

After three days of stimulating and thought-provoking presentations, displays, and discussions, the "Legacy of 1848" conference concluded in Northfield, Minnesota, on April 2, 2017. Sponsored by the Stoltenberg Institute for German-American Forty-Eighter Studies and organized by Drs. Joachim "Yogi" Reppmann (Northfield, Minnesota) and Don Heinrich Tolzmann (Cincinnati, Ohio), the conference attracted speakers, participants, and guests from the United States, Germany, and Denmark.

Always educational and often highly emotional, the conference stimulated everyone to reflect on the challenges that confronted our forebears, how they dealt with and often overcame them, and how mankind can learn and profit from the collective legacy of these brave men and women. As was made obvious to all conference attendees, our ancestors' challenges didn't exist in a vacuum of time, only to disappear at their deaths. Acknowledging these trials, studying their root causes, and familiarizing ourselves with the methods used in combating them, are indispensable for a world where cultural differences are celebrated, not vilified.

Throughout the conference, in echoes of the philosopher George Santayana's statement that "those who cannot remember the past are condemned to repeat it" reverberated throughout Northfield's St. John's Lutheran Church. This famous admonition, which has been thoughtlessly repeated to the point of becoming a mind-numbing bromide, took on new currency throughout "The Legacy of 1848 through Today." As the conference organizers intended, the word "legacy" assumed great importance, for the real and lasting legacy of the influential immigrants of 1848 was their elevation of freedom as the most unifying and integral component in a world community comprised of so many diverse parts.

*****

The conference opened at four o'clock on March 30, 2017, in the conference center of Northfield's lovely St. John's Lutheran Church. After an hour-long welcome reception, where presenters, participants, and attendees re-established old connections and forged new ones, Pastor Klaus Lemke-Paetznick (Wilhelmshaven, Germany) gave an insightful talk about Martin Luther's childhood. This timely presentation — Luther posted his ninety-five theses five hundred years ago on October 31, 1517 — was enhanced by a pictorial exhibit, which chronologically highlighted significant moments in the childhood of the seminal Protestant reformer.

The conference kicked off in earnest at 8:30 on the following morning. Deftly moderated by Dee Eicke, Pastor Lemke-Paetznick, and Dr. Reppmann, the ensuing presentations and discussions of the first day were primarily devoted to Holocaust education. Participants and presenters included Steve Hunegs (executive director, Jewish Community Relations Council for Minnesota and the Dakotas, Minneapolis), Herbert Quelle (German Consul General, Chicago), Carol Kahn-Strauss (Leo Baeck Institute, New York City), Charles Fodor (Hungarian Holocaust survivor), Dr. Gabrielle Robinson (Jewish Federation, South Bend, Indiana), Dr. R. Don Keysser (GACC, Bloomington, Minnesota), Prof. Dr. Gerd-Winand Imeyer (Honorary Consul General of Bulgaria, Hamburg Chamber of Commerce), and Dr. Esther Seha (Minneapolis).

The presentations and discussions were peppered with personal and familial stories, which placed the stain of the Holocaust in a most moving context. Particularly poignant was the presentation of Charles Fodor, who would not have been alive were it not for the chance intercession of a compassionate but nameless individual more than seventy years earlier. Dr. Peter Lubrecht's talk about growing up as a German-American in New York City drove home the point that the repercussions of the Holocaust often migrated across the Atlantic affecting many German-Americans in an insidious, if less visceral way.

After a top-notch keynote address delivered by Chicago's Consul General Herbert Quelle, the evening concluded with the world premiere of Stephan Witthoeft's documentary, *A Flensburg Perspective: Erna de Vries and the Holocaust Boxcar*. This moving film not only highlighted the Holocaust's horrors, but also documented the efforts to bring a Holocaust boxcar (used to transport German Jews to concentration camps) to the *Fagen Fighters World War II Museum* in Granite Falls, Minnesota. Playing a significant role in the acquisition of this important historical artifact was one of the conference's organizers, Dr. Joachim "Yogi" Reppmann. A ninety-eight-page publication chronicling the background of the Holocaust boxcar was also presented to the conference's attendees. The boxcar exhibit at the Fagen museum will be an important and tangible historical reminder that "anyone who does not remember that inhumanity exists, is susceptible to being infected again."

The day concluded with the sixtieth birthday party for conference co-organizer Dr. Yogi Repmann, which was held at Northfield's Froggy Bottoms River Pub. Providing entertainment for the celebration was local guitarist/singer Todd Thompson, who was accompanied by Herbert Quelle on the harmonica. Quelle, a leading German diplomat, recently authored *Monika's Blues*, a book seamlessly weaving the harmonica's importance in the history of blues music with the author's reflections on African-Americans' struggle for freedom.

*****

The second full day of the conference was devoted to the legacy and significance of America's most consequential immigrants, the Forty-Eighters. Enlightening and thought-provoking presentations were given by Dr. Peter Lubrecht (Newton, New Jersey), Prof. Dr. Wolfgang Müller-Michaelis (Hamburg), Felix Zimmermann (Freiburg), Pastor Klaus Lemke-Paetznick (Wilhelmshaven), Jan Jessen (Denmark), Larry Grill (Schleswig, Iowa), conference co-organizer Dr. Don Heinrich Tolzmann (Cincinnati), Dr. Gabrielle Robinson (South Bend, Indiana), Wade Olsen, Denny Warta, and George Glotzbach (New Ulm, Minnesota), Terry Sveine (New Ulm), Dietrich Eicke (Lübeck), Dr. Julie Klassen (Northfield, Minnesota), and Marcus Bracklo (Bad Soden). The presentations and discussions were as interesting as they were varied, with everyone gaining a greater appreciation for the contributions made by the Forty-Eighters and the impressive legacy they bequeathed to subsequent generations.

After a wonderful dinner and genuine fellowship among the conference participants and attendees, Carol Kahn-Strauss (who'd previously received Germany's highest civilian award, the Commander's Cross of the Order of Merit) and Diane Fagen (president of the *Fagen Fighters WWII Museum* in Granite Falls, Minnesota) were presented with the Carl Schurz Award. Both women made heartfelt speeches confirming the soundness of their choice as recipients of the award named in honor of America's most significant and well-known Forty-Eighter, Carl Schurz.

Following this presentation, German Consul General Herbert Quelle (Chicago) presented conference co-organizer Dr. Joachim "Yogi" Reppmann with the German-American Friendship Award of the Federal Republic of Germany for his contributions to German-American relations. As Yogi's friend, I was particularly glad to see him honored in this way. It's long been my view that his outsized personality has often obscured the many real and tangible contributions he's made not only in the historical field, but also in the establishment of bridges furthering contact between and understanding of peoples on both sides of the Atlantic.

*****

The conference concluded with "Thoughts on Being German," a poignant and heartfelt address delivered by Hans Jörg Gudegast, aka Eric Braeden. Born in Bredenbek, Schleswig-Holstein, Gudegast experienced firsthand the horrors of World War II prior to his immigration to the United States in 1959. Energetic, athletic, intellectually inquisitive, and analytical, he fought stereotypes and incredibly long odds to become one of Hollywood's most beloved and well-known stars. He has appeared in scores of movies and TV shows, including thirty-seven years in the signature role of "Victor Newman" on *The Young and the Restless*.

Braeden's experiences and deep understanding provided a fitting denouement for a conference whose first day emphasized the Holocaust. Throughout his adult life, the humanitarian and activist has worked hard in promoting a positive, realistic, and balanced image of German-Americans and advancing German-Jewish dialogue. A man of strong convictions, Braeden believes "Nazi Germany would not have existed had we had a democracy. Had Germany remained a democracy, we wouldn't be talking about the Holocaust. We wouldn't be talking about any of this."

Braeden's life experiences also dovetailed beautifully with the focus of the conference's second day, the important and influential immigrant group known as the Forty-Eighters. Like the Forty-Eighters who were honored at the conference — immigrants who were shocked slavery could exist in a country ostensibly embracing the ideas embodied in the Constitution and Declaration of Independence — Braeden, too, faced similar disillusioning moments. "I came here in 1959. I took the Greyhound bus from New York to Galveston, Texas, to the South, and I thought I had landed in a full democracy, and here I see signs for 'Whites Only,' for 'Coloreds only,' and the separation was stark."

Having spent the better part of the last two decades trying to understand the Forty-Eighters, it's my belief Braeden could well have been a member of this significant immigrant group had he been born 120 years earlier. Like so many of the Forty-Eighters I've studied, Braeden is straightforward, direct — some might even say blunt — yet at the same time, richly nuanced in so many ways. Having lived in America for over half a century, his fervent love for his adopted country has never blinded him to the fact that the struggle to live up to the ideals embodied in our founding documents is a never-ending one requiring constant vigilance. Like so many of the Forty-Eighters, Braeden has never been content to sit on the sidelines. He takes a very active interest in politics and helps rally support for those he feels will best serve the needs of his adopted country.

As a German-American who embraces the best of both cultures, Braeden has devoted much of his time to strengthening the ties between the German and American peoples, and his exemplary efforts in this regard have been honored on many occasions. He's been awarded the Federal Medal of Honor from Germany's President on two separate occasions, been invited to the White House by President Reagan to celebrate German-American Heritage Day, and received the Ellis Island Medal of Honor in 2007.

Yet, as much as Eric Braeden fosters German-American relations and as much as he is a loyal American citizen, he will also always be a German. Having a deep appreciation of, respect for, and loyalty to both countries is an inherent part of the man's complexity. The inherent duality of his life was evidenced time and time again throughout his concluding address, as reflected in the numerous times he had to pause and gather himself while conveying the essence of what it means to an American who will also always be a German.

As Braeden* concluded his talk, I remembered a previous remark of his I'd run across while writing a brief biographical sketch of him some years ago: "I grew up tough. I'll fight you to the last — I'll never give up." What an apropos sentiment for a conference devoted to the study of the Forty-Eighters and Holocaust survivors. It is precisely this trait — that of never giving up, of triumphing over long odds through the sheer force of one's will — that conference attendees and participants celebrated at "The Legacy of 1848 Through Today."   www.Moin-Moin.us

– Scott C. Christiansen, Iowa City

* Joachim Reppmann, *Eric Braeden, From Bredenbek to Hollywood: The Legacy of 1848, Through Today*, Northfield, MN and Flensburg, SH, 2016. (Printing on Demand: www.LuLu.com)

Eric Braeden discussed his "Thoughts on Being German" at the Legacy of 1848 Conference in Northfield, Minnesota; from left: Dee Eicke, Germany; Eric Braeden, Hollywood; Yogi Reppmann, Northfield, MN; and Herbert Quelle, Chicago, Consul General.

Patricia and Don Heinrich Tolzmann coordinated a display of publications dealing with topics covered by the conference.

Biographies of Contributors

Friedhelm (Fiede) Caspari* was born in 1946 near the Mosel River, in the wine region of Rheinland-Pfalz. He had decades of press and media experience from 1968 to 2008, including as a newspaper editor and as North German correspondent of the German Press Agency (dpa), together. In his current freelance journalistic activities he covers historical topics, biographies, business analyses, and the realm of medicine and pharmacy. - In 1988 he took part in the first in a series of U.S. excursions, organized and led by the historian Dr. Joachim "Yogi" Reppmann, under the title "On the Trail of the Schleswig-Holstein Immigrants." Highly motivated since that time, Fiede Caspari has followed the German-American involvement of his friend Yogi and has frequently commented on it in his writings. Born immediately after the crushing of the Nazi dictatorship and the end of the Second World War, Fiede Caspari sees it as his self-evident duty to elucidate those horrific years and not let them fade from memory. In the case of most families, the silence that dominated the Nazi generation and the German participants in the war remained unbroken until subsequent generations. - In the present situation, Caspari has increasingly underscored the unmistakable tendencies toward a growing right-wing extremism that has developed not only in Germany but in the rest of Europe and the United States as well. Definite parallels to the unstable years of democracy in Germany after the First World War cannot be overlooked. An outside observer might well say: nip these early signs in the bud—a burning candle can be extinguished, but not a forest fire.   www.caspari-pr.de

*The name "Caspari," of Italian and/or Roman origin, is not unknown in many cities of the United States. It goes back almost 2,000 years to the Romans' foundation of the city of Trier on the Mosel River and other settlements. The original (Catholic) spelling is Caspary, while the later Protestant and Jewish lines use the form Caspari.

Joachim (Yogi) Reppmann, Ph.D., was born in Flensburg, Schleswig-Holstein, in 1957. He attended Altes Gymnasium, a school founded by Danish King Frederick II in 1566. He matriculated at the University of Kiel, where he studied history and American literature. In 1984, he completed his masters thesis entitled *Transplanted Ideas: The Concept of Freedom and Democracy of the Schleswig-Holstein Forty-Eighters — Origins and Effects 1846-1856*. He has written several books on notable Schleswig-Holstein emigrants and the mass migration to the United States; served as a professor of German at St. Olaf and Carleton Colleges in Northfield, Minnesota; and chaired several conferences on topics ranging from the Low German language to Forty-Eighter Hans Reimer Claussen. Since 1983, Yogi has organized both individualized language study-abroad programs and educational exchanges between the United States and Germany for groups as diverse as farmers from Holstein, Iowa; American teachers of German; college football players; and representatives of the Mayo Clinic in Rochester, Minnesota. Since 2010, the founding of the amazing *German-American Heritage Museum, Washington, DC, www.gahmusa.org*, Yogi has served on its Board. Always looking to strengthen ties between the two areas he calls home — the Baltic Sea region in northern German and America's Midwest — Yogi co-founded *de.us, International Connections* to facilitate and incubate new business connections between the two regions.   www.Moin-Moin.us

The text of the present booklet was translated by **Norman Watt,** Ph.D.. He was born in 1938 in New Jersey, taught German language and literature from 1966 to 2000 at St. Olaf College, Northfield, MN. Main literary interests: German poetry and German and Austrian literature of the late nineteenth and early twentieth centuries; has translated novellas by Arthur Schnitzler and has written a novel, as yet unpublished. May be contacted at: watt@stolaf.edu.

Danke

Erna & Ruth de Vries

Diane & Ron Fagen

Christine Lieberknecht

Marion Schneider

Evelyn Sadri

Carol Kahn Strauss

Henry Kissinger

Peter Prass

Steve Hunegs

Konrad Giessmann

Stephan Witthöft

Thomas Erdmann

Steffen Klosseck

Stephan Richter

Morton Kane

Hanne & Jochen Görrissen

Ameeta Sony & Craig D. Rice

Kenneth Engel

Peter Stoll

Craig L. Rice

Paul Hager

Wayne Eddy

Jeff Johnson

Teri Knight

German-American Heritage Museum

German-American Heritage Museum
719 6th St. NW,
Washington, D.C., 20001, USA
www.gahfusa.org
(202) 467-5000

Please consider a membership for yourself or your loved ones in the German-American Heritage Foundation of the USA, GAHF, which runs a first-rate museum in Washington, D.C. (The museum occupies a former villa owned by a German-American beer brewer and is not far away from the White House). Annual individual membership starts at $50 (Associate Member [non-voting]). Membership includes an informative newsletter on glossy paper, an invitation to a wonderful gala (German-American of the Year), along with exhibits and events, sometimes including a "Frühschoppen" (morning pint) on a weekend!

www.gahmusa.org/product/individual-membership

www.ingramcontent.com/pod-product-compliance
Lightning Source LLC
Chambersburg PA
CBHW081348040426
42450CB00015B/3345